GOD IS MORE THAN ENOUGH

Other books and materials by Jim Berg

Basics for Believers

Changed into His Image

Taking Time to Change

Changed into His Image Student Edition

Transformados en Su Imagen

Created for His Glory

Taking Time to Rejoice

Essential Virtues

Quieting a Noisy Soul Counseling Program

Purity DVD Series

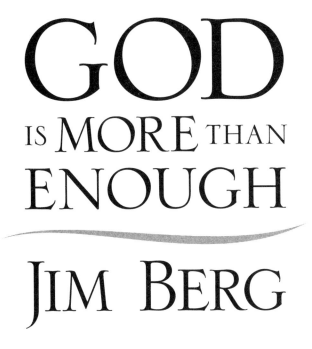

GOD
IS MORE THAN
ENOUGH

JIM BERG

foundations for a quiet soul

journeyforth®

Greenville, South Carolina

Library of Congress Cataloging-in-Publication Data

Berg, Jim, 1952-
   God is more than enough : foundations for a quiet soul / Jim Berg.
      p. cm.
   Includes bibliographical references.
   Summary: "God Is More than Enough is a roadmap of how to use Bible principles to quiet your soul"—Provided by publisher.
   ISBN 978-1-60682-057-5 (perfect bound pbk. : alk. paper)
   1. Spirituality—Biblical teaching. 2. Christian life—Biblical teaching. I. Title.
   BS680.S7B47 2010
   248.8'6—dc22
                                                          2009052348

All Scripture is quoted from the Authorized King James Version unless otherwise noted.

ALMIGHTY, UNCHANGEABLE GOD. Words and Music by Cindy Berry. Copyright © 1996 by GlorySound, a div. of Shawnee Press, Inc. International Copyright Secured. All Rights Reserved. *Reprinted by permission of Hal Leonard Corporation.*

ESV: Scripture quotations marked ESV are from The Holy Bible, English Standard Version®, copyright © 2001 by Crossway Bibles, a publishing ministry of Good News Publishers. Used by permission. All rights reserved.

NASB: Scripture taken from the NEW AMERICAN STANDARD BIBLE®, Copyright © 1960, 1962, 1963, 1968, 1971, 1972, 1973, 1975, 1977, 1995 by The Lockman Foundation. Used by permission.

God Is More than Enough

Design and page layout by Craig Oesterling

© 2010 by BJU Press
Greenville, South Carolina 29614
JourneyForth Books is a division of BJU Press

Printed in the United States of America
All rights reserved

ISBN 978–1–60682–057–5

15 14 13 12 11 10 9 8 7 6 5 4 3 2

This book is dedicated to my grandchildren.

It is my prayer that as they behold their heavenly Father in His Word and see Christ in their parents' lives they will, indeed, find that God is more than enough.

CONTENTS

PREFACE   ix

PART ONE—THE WAY DOWN   xi

    Chapter One   Noticing the Noise in Your Soul   1

    Chapter Two   Unmasking the Source of Your Noise   11

    Chapter Three   Understanding the Solution   22

    Chapter Four   Tracking "The Way Down," Part 1   34

    Chapter Five   Tracking "The Way Down," Part 2   43

PART TWO—THE WAY BACK   57

    Chapter Six   Finding That God Is More than Enough   59

    Chapter Seven   Beholding the God of Love   69

    Chapter Eight   Beholding the God of Mercy   81

    Chapter Nine   Beholding the God of Faithfulness   91

    Chapter Ten   Beholding the God of Power   102

    Chapter Eleven   Beholding the God of Wisdom   111

    Chapter Twelve   Keeping Your Soul Quiet   122

EPILOGUE—WHERE DO YOU GO FROM HERE?   132

APPENDICES   135

    Appendix A   How to Become a Christian   137

    Appendix B   The Stories of Jennie and Anne   140

    Appendix C   The MAP Method of Meditation   154

    Appendix D   Seeking God   156

NOTES   159

INDEX   161

PREFACE

The apostle Paul said that in the last days "perilous times shall come" (2 Timothy 3:1). I believe we are living in those perilous—dangerous—days. These are days of great uncertainty. We face uncertainty in the financial realms of our country. Corporate scandal and increased government programs are costly to everyone. We face uncertainty in the job and financial markets. We face concerns about terrorism and its staggering global economic and military implications.

These are days of social unrest. The homosexual agenda is making inroads into the fabric of our society, and we still face much racial unrest. The family unit continues to disintegrate. We witness a continuing moral decline with a tidal wave of pornography sweeping away the strength of our nation's men and women—both young and old. Divorce, extramarital affairs, premarital affairs, and unmarried couples living together are commonplace. Entertainment is increasingly laced with sensuality, violence, and materialism.

How are people dealing with these "perilous times?" Some are turning to suicide. Others are turning to alcohol, illegal drugs, and psychiatric medications. Others lash out in road rage, drive-by shootings, and killing sprees. Still others distract themselves with a constant bombardment of entertainment, sports, and other activities. We are a culture of people with noisy souls. This book is designed to help you face that noise and become useful to Christ as light and salt in this unstable world, and thereby glorify our great God (Matthew 5:16).

LOOKING AHEAD

This book is divided into two parts.

"Part One—The Way Down" describes how our souls become noisy in the first place.

"Part Two—The Way Back" outlines the major truths about our great God and His gospel, which must be a part of a believer's thinking processes to reverse the noise in our souls.

This book you are reading is an overview of the foundational truths that form the core of the first eleven and the final sessions of *Quieting a Noisy Soul Counseling Program*. This multimedia program contains video and audio sessions of the material in this book along with twelve sessions not covered here. *Quieting a Noisy Soul* also features a study guide, *Taking Time to Quiet Your Soul*, and a meditation/relaxation CD that is of special help to those struggling with anxiety, depression, and other destructive issues. For a full description of the counseling program, see pages 132–33 or go to www.QuietingaNoisySoul.com.

God Is More than Enough can serve as a ready review and reference tool for your own growth in Christ and for your ministry to others. It is useful as an introductory text to biblical counseling as well. Those using this book in small groups or Sunday school programs will find the Take Time to Reflect section at the end of each chapter helpful to stimulate application and group discussion.

Consider this book a roadmap of how to quiet your soul. The twenty-four-week personal counseling program actually takes you on the journey. With this understanding behind us, we can spread out the roadmap and look at the highways we need to travel.

PART ONE

THE WAY DOWN

Chapter One

NOTICING THE NOISE IN YOUR SOUL

Come unto me, all ye that labour and are heavy laden, and I will give you rest. Take my yoke upon you, and learn of me; for I am meek and lowly in heart: and ye shall find rest unto your souls. For my yoke is easy [tailor-made], and my burden is light. (Matthew 11:28–30)

Have you ever stood on the bank of a slow moving river or a still pond and thrown a rock into its tranquil surface? If you have, you saw concentric circles of waves move away from the place where the stone entered the water. Noise in the physical realm consists of similar waves though they are invisible.

Noise in the soul, however, consists of *thoughts*. If we are going to quiet the noise in our souls, we will have to examine our thoughts. Most people can immediately tell you how they *feel* about something, but they are not very aware of their thoughts. If we are going to quiet the noise in our souls, *we will have to track our thinking not our feelings*, and then we must evaluate those thoughts against the Word of God. Where our thoughts are wrong, we must repent of them and replace them with thoughts that honor God. We must know, therefore, what the wrong kind of thoughts look like and face them biblically.

WHAT DOES NOISE IN THE SOUL SOUND LIKE?

Jesus gave us some clues about what noise in the soul sounds like in Matthew 11:28–30—the passage printed at the top of this page. These verses are the prototype of peace. This passage tells us how to have peace *with* God and how to have the peace *of* God.

The congregation Jesus was addressing was probably broader than just His disciples. Perhaps the assembly was made up of Pharisees and other

1

religious leaders who had come to listen to Him. The crowd probably also consisted of many people who had been listening to the Pharisees tell them that they had to do all sorts of things to be at peace with God. They had noisy souls trying to obtain salvation. Jesus' call to His followers was to come and learn from Him how to have lasting rest and peace. If you are not sure that you possess eternal life yourself, please go to appendix A to find out "How to Become a Christian."

Jesus said to them all, "Come unto me, all ye that labour." The word *labour* means "to grow weary, to be beaten out." The root word means to take a beating.[1] Most of us identify with that. We have at times felt overwhelmed as if we were in a hurricane with the winds pounding unceasingly against our souls. It is to us in those times that Jesus says, "Come to Me; I can help people like that."

The words *heavy laden* mean burdened down like a ship loaded with cargo.[2] We all know what it is like to feel that we cannot take the pressure any longer; we feel as though we are about to go under. Again, Jesus says, "Come to Me; I can help people like that." What a wonderful invitation He extends to us! He wants us to come to Him; He wants to help!

I want you to take an inventory of the noises in your soul—the things that rob you of rest and peace. Before you do that, however, notice a passage written by David in Psalm 40:1–2. He says, "I waited patiently for the Lord; and *he inclined unto me, and heard my cry*" (emphasis mine).

Notice carefully the words in italics in that verse. Did you know that God's inclination is to hear you? You might say, "I've got so many problems, God doesn't want to listen to me." No, if you have many problems, He *wants* to listen to you. David said further, "He heard my cry." He will hear your cry too.

David goes on to say, "He brought me up also out of an horrible pit." The words *horrible pit* literally mean "a pit of noise." Maybe you, too, feel as though you are in a pit of noise. Do you know what God wants to do? Listen to David in Psalm 40:2–3.

> [He] set my feet upon a rock, and established my goings. And he hath put a new song in my mouth, even praise unto our God: many shall see it, and fear, and shall trust in the Lord.

God wants to set your feet on a rock. He wants to give you stability. He wants to "establish your goings." That is, He wants to direct your ways so that when others look at your life they see what God is doing and want the same thing for themselves.

So, let's get started inventorying your thoughts—noticing the noise in your soul.

Are there sounds of anxiety and fear in your soul?

Anxious thoughts are thoughts of worry: "What if this happens, and what if that happens?" These are thoughts of vulnerability and uncertainty: "I can't lose control of this, and so-and-so is doing that, and I can't let that happen either." "This is going on over there, and I have to be sure that turns out right. I must not let anything go out of control."

Are there sounds of discouragement and despair in your soul?

These are thoughts of hopelessness: "What's the use? I may as well give up. There is no hope. It will not get any better. It will always be this way." What about thoughts of defeat? "I blew it again. I'll never get on top of this. I'm always failing. I never can have lasting victory." Despair thrives on thoughts of self-pity: "This always happens to me. Nobody else goes through this. I always get the short end of the stick. I never get any breaks."

Are there sounds of anger and frustration in your soul?

Anger is generally fueled by frustration, hurt, or fear. Check your thoughts. Are you thinking things like "I can't believe that happened again. That should have been straightened out the last time. Is it too much to ask that these things get solved once and for all?" These are frustrated, agitated thoughts. Angry thoughts rise up when someone hurts us by something he has said or done or when we are put into a vulnerable position.

Are there sounds of bitterness and hatred in your soul?

These are thoughts of injustice, mistreatment, and unfairness: "I've poured my life into this job/marriage, and I get treated like dirt! That's not fair!" Sometimes these are thoughts of contempt or revenge: "I won't let that happen again. I'll get him back some way. Nobody is going to get away with that."

Are there sounds of lust and greed in your soul?

Is your mind filled with thoughts of illicit pleasure and experiences—things that you know you should not be indulging in and lusting for? You create noise in your soul when you plan to get the pleasure you want and then plan its cover-up. Is your mind filled with covetous thoughts? You look at what the world has to offer and you can't seem to stop thinking about some new fashion, gadget, automobile, house, or some other item you think you must have to be happy. The more time you spend comparing prices and comparing yourself with others, the more discontent—and noisy—your soul becomes.

Are there sounds of guilt and shame in your soul?

Anytime you practice the kinds of thoughts we have been discussing above, you will generate thoughts of guilt and shame because God never intended you to think that way. He has marvelous provisions for us to deal with these matters. He weighs our conscience down with great burdens when we sin. In fact, the noise of a guilty conscience is the loudest noise you can have because of the danger of being out of fellowship with God. This is the noise of sinfulness, remorse, and embarrassment.

Are there sounds of possessions and positions in your soul?

Our souls can get very noisy with the daily responsibilities of being a husband or wife, parent, employee, employer, church leader, and so forth. Our minds can be filled with thoughts of our to-do lists and strategies we are planning. Some of the noise might be from thoughts of ambition, trying to get ahead, be on top, get the latest and greatest possessions, or simply trying to get it all done or to maintain the possessions we have.

Are there sounds of obsessions and addictions in your soul?

These thoughts lead a person into drugs, alcohol, binging and purging, self-starvation, self-mutilation, pornography, theft, illicit affairs, lying, sexual abuse, and so forth. In addition to the guilt, the planning, cover-up, rationalization, rituals, and self-imposed demands generate an enormous amount of noise.

Are there sounds of entertainment and recreation in your soul?

These are thoughts of movies and TV programs, of music and news, of sports and electronic games, of travels and adventures. In our connected age we have the opportunity to fill our minds with distractions 24/7, at lightning speed, and over hundreds of channels and unlimited texts and posts. How many times have we come home from a strenuous day, and rather than spending some time reflecting upon what God wants to do in our lives through our difficulties that day, we do something to escape the responsibility for our poor responses of the day? We find something that will make us feel good. We watch a movie and fill our minds with more noise for three hours. When it is over, we replay in our minds certain scenes and think about how the plot unfolded. We have just succeeded in generating more noise!

If we've had a difficult day, it would be better if we sat down quietly and asked, "God, why was this day so joyless for me?" This is not the time to fill our minds with more noise. It is the time to reflect: "God what is so wrong with my heart that I missed what You are trying to do in me today?"

As you can see, the collective noise from these thoughts is deafening! How different these scenes are from the way the Master wants His disciples to handle life. Jesus had much to do on the earth, but His soul wasn't noisy. He wasn't irritated and saying, "Now, Peter, did you get that done? John, did you check on that? Andrew—oh, where is Andrew? He's never around when I need him. What on earth am I going to do with Andrew? Has anyone seen Andrew?" His soul wasn't agitated; it wasn't noisy.

Here is what Jesus told His disciples—and us—in John 14:27 just before He left the scene and put them in charge of propagating His teachings:

> Peace I leave with you, my peace I give unto you [the kind of peace you have seen in Me]: not as the world giveth, give I unto you [You won't get My peace the same way the world tries to get peace]. Let not your heart be troubled, neither let it be afraid.

This is instructive to us. Are you trying to get peace the same way the world tries to get it? The world tries to get peace by filling life with distractions, possessions, adventures, and people. They try all sorts of things as anesthesia to dull the pain of their emptiness. But the Master says, "Not as the world giveth, give I unto you."

All this self-imposed agitation—all this noise—is a sign of spiritual dysfunction and sinful responses. God-centered souls are not noisy. *God-centered souls are at rest.*

WHAT ARE THE DANGERS OF NOISE IN THE SOUL?

First of all, a noisy soul is destructive to the body. It is interesting how many times in Proverbs God talks about how our heart affects our body.[3] Stress-related illnesses and stress-induced complications to physical diseases are the result of noisy souls. Unrestrained and unbiblical thoughts keep the autonomic nervous system activated. Keeping our bodies in emergency mode imposes an enormous strain on them. *Adrenaline is a wonderful friend in a real emergency, but it is a deadly foe as a way of life.* Many of God's people live with high levels of adrenaline because they are always pushing. *Push* is a bad four-letter word when it comes to health. *Rest* is a good four-letter word. Many gastrointestinal disorders, cardiac difficulties, autoimmune system and endocrine dysfunctions, and sleep disorders are related directly to wrongly handled pressure.

Noisy souls also suffer spiritually since noise reflects alienation from God because of sinful responses. We have lost our God-ward gaze. We no longer look at God and seek His direction. We do not see Him as our Savior; we are trying to save ourselves—trying to work out our own problems without His wisdom. This independence from God is not merely a matter of poor judgment that results in ineffectiveness and unrest. It is, rather, mutinous for created beings to turn to themselves for solutions when they were created to depend upon God Himself.[4]

When I was in junior high in South Dakota, a couple of friends and I would ride our bicycles to Joe Foss Field in Sioux Falls, a few miles from my house. It was the municipal airport but had been an air force base during WWII. It housed a squadron of Air National Guard planes. We loved watching those F-102 jets take off and land. We would go home and try to carve model jets out of wood. This was before the days of concern about noise abatement, and the chainlink fence we stood behind wasn't very far from the runway. It was thrilling to watch a jet take off. It was also deafening! We could not even hear each other talk.

That is what noise in the soul can be like. It can be so deafening that we no longer hear the voice of God.

WHAT IS GOD'S CURE FOR NOISE IN THE SOUL?

Matthew 11:28–30 teaches a very wonderful cure. The One we have sinned against—the One Who went to a cross to die for us—says, "Come unto Me." It is a call to fellowship. He says, "I want you to be back in fellowship with Me. I want there to be much going on between us. Come back to Me."

You and I can have a heart that is oriented to God. This is a call to a God-ward gaze, which is the essence of faith whereby we turn away from ourselves and our homemade strategies and look to God for strength, wisdom, deliverance, and hope. It is the opposite of a self-dependent focus.

Listen to His invitation in John 15:4–5. "I want you back. I want to produce fruit in you."

> Abide in me, and I in you. As the branch cannot bear fruit of itself, except it abide in the vine; no more can ye, except ye abide in me. I am the vine, ye are the branches: He that abideth in me, and I in him, the same bringeth forth much fruit: for without me ye can do nothing.

Proverbs 3:5–8 warns us of forsaking the Lord to go our own way.

> Trust in the Lord with all thine heart; and lean not unto thine own understanding. In all thy ways acknowledge him, and he shall direct thy paths. Be not wise in thine own eyes: fear the Lord, and depart from evil. It shall be health to thy navel [your whole body], and marrow [medicine, refreshment] to thy bones.

When we depart from God and break fellowship with Him, we experience the noise we have been talking about because of our sinful responses to life's challenges. We can think of it this way:

> Avoid Me all you that labor and are heavy laden, and I will deny you rest. Refuse My yoke of fellowship and abiding, and refuse to learn what I am like in order to become like Me, and you shall find noise in your soul. (Matthew 11:28–30 Reversed Standard Version)

Instead, the Master says, "Come to Me" for fellowship, and then, "Come and be like Me." This is a call to discipleship. He says, "Take my yoke upon you and learn of me; for I am meek and lowly in heart."

We cannot cure the noise in our souls by distractions or by recreations or by medications. Jesus said the cure is meditation. "Come unto Me, and learn of Me." A focused, deliberate gaze upon Christ and His ways is the solution. He says, "Come learn of Me, for I am meek. I want you to be like Me—willing to be governed." Meekness strikes at the heart of our pride. We do not want to be governed.

The godfather of noisemakers is pride. Most of our noise is created when we try to gain control of our lives, or regain control when it has been taken away. We are constantly fighting our limitations and our restrictions. This is not meekness; this is not a willingness to be governed. This fight for control is a major source of noise and pressure.

Pride whines and pouts; pride shouts and demands; pride argues and debates; pride covets and grasps; pride screams and retaliates; pride shifts blame and points fingers; pride lusts and indulges; pride manipulates and schemes; pride drives and obsesses; pride worries and frets. That is a lot of noise!

Pride is full of self-assertion, self-protection, self-promotion, self-confidence, and self-esteem. Pride cries out, "I will not! I must have! I don't have to . . . ! I won't let that happen! I can't take any more of . . . ! I don't like this!" This is not meekness; these are the sounds of a noisy soul!

Self is a relentless noisemaker, like a hungry unweaned child on his mother's lap. Psalm 131 is a beautiful picture. David declares, "I have calmed and quieted my soul, like a weaned child with its mother; like a weaned child is my soul within me" (Psalm 131:2 ESV).

When a hungry, nursing child gets anywhere near his mother, he is squirming and nudging. He is fussy; he is restless because he wants to nurse. David says, "I've learned to quiet my soul. I'm satisfied; I'm not fussy."

Are you willing to repent of the responses that leave God out and generate noise in your soul? Are you willing to be content with what God is doing in your life? Are you willing to be meek—to be governed by

God? Matthew 11 tells us that Jesus is "meek." You must learn meekness from Him.

Jesus also says, "I want you to be lowly in heart like Me." He wants us to be humble. This humility is at the heart of the meekness. Jesus' life was not about Himself. He said, "Learn from Me; I am your pattern."

If you read through John's Gospel, you will see Jesus saying things such as "I did not come down here to do My own will, but the will of My Father. I came to accomplish His work" (5:30; 9:4). He said to His disciples, "What shall I say? That I shouldn't suffer? No! This is why I came" (12:27). He was willing to be humble and do what His Father wanted Him to do.

Our fussiness and agitation exist because we have our own agenda, and other people aren't getting into step with it. But we are not here on this earth to do our own work; we are here, just like Jesus, to do the work of our Father. If we are humble, we will have a constant spirit of repentance and dependence in us. We will have a continual spirit of deference and service to others.

What about you? Do you have a noisy soul? What sounds—what thoughts—fill your soul? Do you hear the voice of the Lord Jesus calling you to come to Him?

You may say, "But my life is such a mess. I've been this way twenty years. I don't know if I can be helped." You are the one Jesus is talking about when He says, "Come unto Me all of you who are laboring and heavily loaded down."

What I want you to notice in this first chapter is the extent to which your soul is filled with noise, and the amazing disposition our Lord has toward you. He wants you to come back.

Are you willing to say to God, "I'm willing to lay down my noisemakers. I'm willing to lay down my pride, repent of my sinful responses, and I'm coming back to You"? Are you willing to learn from Him? I hope that is your prayer as we go through this study.

I would ask you to pray something like this every time you come to this study: "Lord, show me anything You want me to do and with Your help—Your grace—I'll do it." *You must come to Christ and purpose to be like Him to quiet the noise in your soul.*

Take Time to Reflect

In Matthew 11:28 Jesus says, "Come unto me, all ye that labour [are beaten down] and are heavy laden [burdened down], and I will give you rest." Take a few moments to reflect upon your life. What comes to your mind under these two categories? How do they describe your situation currently or recently?

1. "Beaten down" [i.e., to take a beating; to be weary]

2. "Burdened down" [i.e., like a heavily loaded ship]

3. Is the heart of the Lord Jesus, revealed in Matthew 11:28, what you have envisioned His heart toward you? If not, what is different about what He says is His heart toward you and what you think it is?

Chapter Two

UNMASKING THE SOURCE
OF YOUR NOISE

*Grace and peace be multiplied unto you through the knowledge of God,
and of Jesus our Lord, according as his divine power hath given unto us
all things that pertain unto life and godliness, through the knowledge of
him that hath called us to glory and virtue. (2 Peter 1:2–3)*

Where do we start in our noise-abatement efforts? As you may have
noticed in the verses above, Peter says that multiplied peace has something to do with the knowledge of God—the truth about God. Therefore, in some way our noise problem is related to the absence of this
knowledge—the absence of what is true about God in our belief
system—in our heart.

THE NATURE OF TRUTH

Truth has always been important, but in our postmodern, relativistic age,
it is even more crucial for us to underscore some basics. Paul teaches us
that there are certain things every man knows to be true. According to
Romans 1:19–20 the existence of God and His great power are "clearly
seen" and "understood" by the creation—so much so that every man is
"without excuse" when it comes to knowing that God exists.

The problem according to verse 21 is that man willfully refuses to acknowledge God's existence and/or rulership over him and thereby begins the process of his own disintegration. He exchanges what he knows
to be true about God for a lie (1:25). He can't exchange something he
does not possess. He *does* know certain things to be true about God but
must reject them, sentencing himself to his own deception.

Stability exists only upon a foundation of truth. So, let's first start with a simple definition of truth.

Truth is that which corresponds to reality.

When you were young, you probably heard around Christmastime about a rather large man dressed in a red coat trimmed in white fur, who delivered presents to good little children all around the world on Christmas Eve. He accomplished this by going from house to house in a sleigh pulled by flying reindeer and entered each house through the chimney. Somehow he knew who was good and who was bad, and he knew what each boy or girl wanted for Christmas.

You probably also heard at Christmas about a baby boy born in Bethlehem to a virgin mother newly espoused to her husband, Joseph. An angel had told her that His name was to be called Jesus, for He would save His people from their sins.

We might entertain little children with the first story of Santa Claus, but we readily acknowledge that it is not true because none of its components correspond to reality. Presents cannot be delivered by one man to that many children on one evening, reindeer do not fly, large men cannot get down chimneys, and no one person can know which children have been good or bad.

The second story is true because it corresponds precisely to reality. Jesus *was* born of a virgin in Bethlehem. Mary *was* His human mother though Joseph was not His father.

This distinction between reality and fantasy is crucial to everything we will see in the chapters ahead. Our responses to life's circumstances must be based upon *reality*—what is true about God and life as He has revealed it to us.

The opposite of reality is *fantasy*—make-believe stories based upon our imagination. Most of us have rejected certain realities of God and have believed fantasies about God more than we realize. If you have a noisy soul, you probably will be quite shocked—and perhaps shaken—to see in the chapters ahead how much your view of God is not anchored in reality.

There is a corollary to our definition of truth that we also want to consider.

Nothing can be true and untrue at the same time.

The existence of Santa Claus as the popular myth reports cannot be true and untrue at the same time. Either reindeer really do fly or they don't. Either large men can get down chimneys or they cannot.

In a similar fashion it cannot be true that God cares about you and me and also be true that God does not care about you and me. The Bible reveals to us the truth about God. He exists as a certain kind of person in all ages, in all places, and to everyone. He is forever the same (Hebrews 13:8). He does not have good days and bad days. He does not have favorite children and children He tolerates because He has to.

Please understand that this is more than mere philosophical wrangling. *Understanding these facts about reality is a major factor in determining whether your life brings glory to God and whether you yourself are a faith-filled and stable person.* It is crucial to the noise reduction in your soul. Let's take this one step further.

THE DANGER OF UNBELIEF

First, let's look at a definition of a belief.

A belief is what you accept to be true.

Some children believe in Santa Claus even though he doesn't exist with all the powers of the man in the story. *Miracle on 34th Street* notwithstanding, if they hold on to this belief into adult life, they will encounter many difficulties making life work and maintaining personal credibility.

Other children grow up believing "Jesus loves me this I know; For the Bible tells me so." If they undergird that belief with the realities about God that they find in the Bible, they will become unusually stable and highly useful in God's mission on the earth.

The point here is that you can believe something about Santa Claus—or God—that is not true. To the extent that your beliefs are grounded in reality, your life will have stability and will honor God. To the extent that your beliefs are rooted in fantasy, you will be unstable, will dishonor God, and will experience many unpleasant surprises as you try to live out your fantasy in real life.

Let's look at one more definition.

Unbelief is rejecting what God says is true.

What we must understand is that we are always believing someone; nonbelief is nonexistent. You either believe your own ideas about how the world is ordered and about the kind of person God is or you believe what God has said in the Bible about Himself and the world He created.

Unbelief—rejecting what God says is true—is problematic for two reasons. First and most seriously, rejecting the truth about God is a highhanded insult against God Himself; it dishonors Him (Romans 1:21, 25). It treats God as if He is a liar and is not truthful about what He has said about Himself and about the way life works in the world He created. This is a horrible offense against God.

Secondly, rejecting the truth about God begins the process of your own disintegration (Romans 1:21–32). A person who insists on living in a fantasy world that does not correspond to reality will encounter many bumps on the road and will have no idea why life is so difficult.

Consider these statements of unbelief:

- "You cannot trust anyone—not even God. You must look out for yourself."

- "God doesn't love me or He wouldn't have messed up my life by putting me in this family."

- "If I marry a loving spouse and have lots of money, I'll be happy."

You can certainly sense the pain in the first two statements and feel the optimism in the last one, but none of these statements is true. A person who goes through life believing these statements is experiencing a serious break with reality. The truth is God is always trustworthy and God always loves us and a loving spouse and lots of money do not guarantee happiness at all. A person who rejects the truth and believes a lie about God or anything else in God's world will experience personal disintegration and, furthermore, cannot live a life honoring to God because he rejects what God says is true.

You must labor to find out what is true according to God, repent of believing anything else, resolutely reject any deviation from it, and cling to the things that are true about God no matter what happens to you.

This is the source of Job's stability during astonishing pressures. He knew that certain things about God were true, and he would not disbelieve them no matter what! (See Job 1:20–22; 2:9–10; 13:15).

THE GLORY OF GOD

What is at stake here ultimately is not our unhappiness and disintegration but the glory of God. Unbelief robs God of His glory (Romans 1:21). His unique excellence is tarnished in our view. He becomes in our mind no better than the creatures He made—weak, untrustworthy, unloving, unkind, and unwise. Those descriptors fit us; they do not fit God! The temptation of the sinful heart is to "[exchange] the truth of God [for] a lie" (Romans 1:25). We must repent of this position and seek forgiveness from God Himself for He is the One we have wronged by our unbelief.

The source of our noise is this unbelief; the solution is repentance and a renewed mind—a Spirit-illuminated vision from the Scriptures of Who God is. Remember what Peter said: "Grace and peace be multiplied unto you *through the knowledge of God*" (2 Peter 1:2, emphasis mine).

STABILIZING TRUTHS FOR NOISY SOULS: THE KNOWLEDGE OF GOD

The following statements are truths straight from God Himself about Himself. They form the bedrock of stable living and of a life that glorifies God.

Labor, labor, labor to *know* these truths—look up the verses and find other verses of Scripture that teach these truths. *Memorize* these truths and the verses that support them (Psalm 119:9–11). *Meditate* upon these truths (1 Timothy 4:15–16). Fellowship with others about these truths (1 John 1:3). Test every stray thought of your heart by these truths (2 Corinthians 10:3–5), and don't despise preaching about these truths (2 Timothy 4:2–4). To reject them is to believe a lie and to begin the process of your own disintegration.

Prayerfully and reflectively read these brief statements about God and the Scripture passages that support them. Write the heading on the top of an index card (i.e., "He will always meet my genuine needs—always.") and then write out the text of the supporting verses below the heading.[1] Carry the card with you and begin memorizing and meditating upon that truth throughout the day. We will explore several of these truths in more detail in the chapters to follow.

1. God is always good—always! That means . . .

   a. He will always meet my genuine needs—always!

> I can do all things through Christ which strengtheneth me. . . . But my God shall supply all your need according to his riches in glory by Christ Jesus. (Philippians 4:13, 19)

> Therefore take no thought, saying, What shall we eat? or, What shall we drink? or, Wherewithal shall we be clothed? (For after all these things do the Gentiles seek:) for your heavenly Father knoweth that ye have need of all these things. But seek ye first the kingdom of God, and his righteousness; and all these things shall be added unto you. (Matthew 6:31–33)

   b. He will always forgive my sin—always!

> If we confess our sins, he is faithful and just to forgive us our sins, and to cleanse us from all unrighteousness. (1 John 1:9)

> Have mercy upon me, O God, according to thy lovingkindness: according unto the multitude of thy tender mercies blot out my transgressions. Wash me throughly from mine iniquity, and cleanse me from my sin. For I acknowledge my transgressions: and my sin is ever before me. Against thee, thee only, have I sinned, and done this evil in thy sight: that thou mightest be justified when thou speakest, and be clear when thou judgest. Behold, I was shapen in iniquity; and in sin did my mother conceive me. Behold, thou desirest truth in the inward parts: and in the hidden part thou shalt make me to know wisdom. Purge me with hyssop, and I shall be clean: wash me, and I shall be whiter than snow. Make me to hear joy and gladness; that the bones which thou hast broken may rejoice. Hide thy face from my sins, and blot out all mine iniquities. Create in me a clean heart, O God; and renew a right spirit within me. Cast me not away from thy presence; and take not thy holy spirit from me. Restore unto me the joy of thy salvation; and uphold me with thy free spirit. Then will I teach transgressors thy ways; and sinners shall be converted unto thee. Deliver me from bloodguiltiness, O God, thou God of my salvation: and my tongue shall sing aloud of thy righteousness. O Lord, open thou my lips; and my mouth shall shew forth thy praise. For thou desirest not sacrifice; else would I give it: thou delightest not

in burnt offering. The sacrifices of God are a broken spirit: a broken and a contrite heart, O God, thou wilt not despise. Do good in thy good pleasure unto Zion: build thou the walls of Jerusalem. Then shalt thou be pleased with the sacrifices of righteousness, with burnt offering and whole burnt offering: then shall they offer bullocks upon thine altar. (Psalm 51)

To this man will I look, even to him that is poor and of a contrite spirit, and trembleth at my word. (Isaiah 66:2*b*)

c. He is always up to something good in my life—always!

For I know the thoughts that I think toward you, saith the Lord, thoughts of peace, and not of evil, to give you an expected end. (Jeremiah 29:11)

Likewise the Spirit also helpeth our infirmities: for we know not what we should pray for as we ought: but the Spirit itself maketh intercession for us with groanings which cannot be uttered. And he that searcheth the hearts knoweth what is the mind of the Spirit, because he maketh intercession for the saints according to the will of God. And we know that all things work together for good to them that love God, to them who are the called according to his purpose. For whom he did foreknow, he also did predestinate to be conformed to the image of his Son, that he might be the firstborn among many brethren. Moreover whom he did predestinate, them he also called: and whom he called, them he also justified: and whom he justified, them he also glorified. What shall we then say to these things? If God be for us, who can be against us? He that spared not his own Son, but delivered him up for us all, how shall he not with him also freely give us all things? Who shall lay any thing to the charge of God's elect? It is God that justifieth. Who is he that condemneth? It is Christ that died, yea rather, that is risen again, who is even at the right hand of God, who also maketh intercession for us. (Romans 8:26–34)

d. He will always love me personally—always!

Who shall separate us from the love of Christ? shall tribulation, or distress, or persecution, or famine, or nakedness, or peril, or sword? As it is written, For thy sake we are killed all the day long; we are accounted as sheep for the slaughter. Nay, in all these things we are more than conquerors through him that loved us. For I am persuaded, that neither death, nor life, nor angels, nor principalities, nor powers, nor things present, nor things to come, nor height, nor depth, nor any other creature, shall be able to separate us from the love of God, which is in Christ Jesus our Lord. (Romans 8:35–39)

The Lord hath appeared of old unto me, saying, Yea, I have loved thee with an everlasting love: therefore with lovingkindness have I drawn thee. (Jeremiah 31:3)

And this is life eternal, that they might know thee the only true God, and Jesus Christ, whom thou hast sent. (John 17:3)

e. He will always give me the grace I need—always!

And God is able to make all grace abound toward you; that ye, always having all sufficiency in all things, may abound to every good work. (2 Corinthians 9:8)

But by the grace of God I am what I am: and his grace which was bestowed upon me was not in vain; but I laboured more abundantly than they all: yet not I, but the grace of God which was with me. (1 Corinthians 15:10)

And he said unto me, My grace is sufficient for thee: for my strength is made perfect in weakness. Most gladly therefore will I rather glory in my infirmities, that the power of Christ may rest upon me. Therefore I take pleasure in infirmities, in reproaches, in necessities, in persecutions, in distresses for Christ's sake: for when I am weak, then am I strong. (2 Corinthians 12:9–10)

2. God is always great—always! That means . . .

a. He is always in control of all things—always!

The Lord hath prepared his throne in the heavens; and his kingdom ruleth over all. (Psalm 103:19)

For the Lord of hosts hath purposed, and who shall disannul it? and his hand is stretched out, and who shall turn it back? (Isaiah 14:27)

Remember the former things of old: for I am God, and there is none else; I am God, and there is none like me, declaring the end from the beginning, and from ancient times the things that are not yet done, saying, My counsel shall stand, and I will do all my pleasure. (Isaiah 46:9–10)

b. He is always present with me—always!

> Whither shall I go from thy spirit? or whither shall I flee from thy presence? If I ascend up into heaven, thou art there: if I make my bed in hell, behold, thou art there. If I take the wings of the morning, and dwell in the uttermost parts of the sea; even there shall thy hand lead me, and thy right hand shall hold me. If I say, Surely the darkness shall cover me; even the night shall be light about me. Yea, the darkness hideth not from thee; but the night shineth as the day: the darkness and the light are both alike to thee. (Psalm 139:7–12)

> Fear thou not; for I am with thee: be not dismayed; for I am thy God: I will strengthen thee; yea, I will help thee; yea, I will uphold thee with the right hand of my righteousness. (Isaiah 41:10)

> Can any hide himself in secret places that I shall not see him? saith the Lord. Do not I fill heaven and earth? saith the Lord. (Jeremiah 23:24)

c. He is always the same—always!

> For I am the Lord, I change not; therefore ye sons of Jacob are not consumed. (Malachi 3:6)

> And, thou, Lord, in the beginning hast laid the foundation of the earth; and the heavens are the works of thine hands: they shall perish; but thou remainest; and they all shall wax old as doth a garment; and as a vesture shalt thou fold them up, and they shall be changed: but thou art the same, and thy years shall not fail. (Hebrews 1:10–12)

d. He is always trustworthy—always!

> If we believe not, yet he abideth faithful: he cannot deny himself. (2 Timothy 2:13)

> Thy mercy, O Lord, is in the heavens; and thy faithfulness reacheth unto the clouds. (Psalm 36:5)

> God is not a man, that he should lie; neither the son of man, that he should repent: hath he said, and shall he not do it? or hath he spoken, and shall he not make it good? (Numbers 23:19)

> Know therefore that the Lord thy God, he is God, the faithful God, which keepeth covenant and mercy with them that love him

and keep his commandments to a thousand generations. (Deuteronomy 7:9)

And the Lord, he it is that doth go before thee; he will be with thee, he will not fail thee, neither forsake thee: fear not, neither be dismayed. (Deuteronomy 31:8)

e. He is always wise in what He does—always!

O the depth of the riches both of the wisdom and knowledge of God! how unsearchable are his judgments, and his ways past finding out! (Romans 11:33)

In whom are hid all the treasures of wisdom and knowledge. (Colossians 2:3)[2]

We must know and believe what is true about God for God cannot be always good and sometimes not good. God cannot always be in control and sometimes not in control. God cannot be always trustworthy and sometimes not trustworthy.

We cannot tolerate unbelief in our souls!

Unbelief will rob God of His glory, begin the process of our own disintegration, and generate much noise in our souls. This is why Solomon said in Proverbs 4:23, "Keep thy heart with all diligence; for out of it are the issues of life." You must guard your heart against unbelief.

Unbelief is the primary cause of the noise in your soul. You do not yet see that God Himself is more than enough for you.

You must know what is true about God and never waiver from it no matter what is happening to you. You must repent of unbelief if you have accepted views of God that are not true, and you must renew your commitment to labor at knowing the truth. The truth about God as revealed in the Scriptures will unmask the source of the noise in your soul.

Take Time to Reflect

1. According to 2 Peter 1:2 how does God increase (i.e., "multiply") our peace?

2. Write out the definition of truth as given in this chapter.

3. Which "Stabilizing Truth" is especially meaningful to you? Why?

Chapter Three

UNDERSTANDING THE SOLUTION

Though our outward man perish, yet the inward man is renewed day by day. For our light affliction, which is but for a moment, worketh for us a far more exceeding and eternal weight of glory; while we look not at the things which are seen, but at the things which are not seen: for the things which are seen are temporal; but the things which are not seen are eternal. (2 Corinthians 4:16b–18)

We have learned that a mind renewed by the Spirit of God with the truth of God is the only antidote to guilt, anxiety, anger, and despair. It is the only cure for a noisy soul.

UNDERSTANDING PRESSURE AND STRAIN

It is important for us to understand how unbelief affects our mind and our body as we face the pressures of life. In order to avoid confusion I'm not going to use the word *stress* in our initial discussion here because the word is used in a popular sense for both the cause and the effect of something. We will hear someone say, "I am stressed today," speaking of the effect of his day, and someone else will say, "I'm under a lot of stress today," using the word as the cause. I'm not calling for a boycott on the word; it just isn't helpful to us as we try to unpack the dynamics of what is going on. Technically, "stress" would apply to the effect of a "stressor"—a cause.

First, we must recognize that *any pressure of life is first evaluated by the mind.* The mind is represented by the top beam of the bridge (see figure 1).

Think of it this way. When you get a bill in the mail from your local power company, you look at your checkbook to see if you have enough money in the bank to cover the check you are about to write to the utility company. Your *mind* does the calculations (if you're like me, you also need a calculator), and if you have enough resources to cover the check, your mind is at rest.

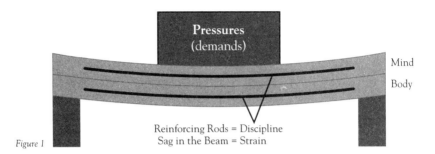

Reinforcing Rods = Discipline
Sag in the Beam = Strain

Figure 1

If, however, you have only $100 in your checking account, and the power bill is for considerably more, your mind may not be at rest. You may become anxious, frustrated, and perhaps even angry or discouraged. You may even feel guilty if you spent money on something you really didn't need, thus depleting your account.

If you do not resolve this dilemma in your mind—in the manner to be discussed later in this chapter—you can expect eventually that this kind of anxiety will have debilitating effects upon your body—the second beam. *Pressure that is not adequately handled in the mind will be borne by the body.*

While most of the following effects can have other causes, they are common indications of bodily strain caused by wrongly handled pressures: muscular tensions and headaches; insomnia and fatigue; increased or decreased appetite; heart palpitations, tics, and itching; colitis, diarrhea, ulcers, cramps, and other stomach disorders; and so forth.

The negative effects of unresolved pressures on the mind and its emotions include the following: depression, boredom, listlessness, dullness, and lack of interest; irritability and "touchiness"; phobias (irrational fears) and anxiety-related disorders (panic attacks, etc.); compulsive behavior (extreme perfectionism, eating disorders, self-mutilation, and excessive cleanliness, orderliness, or exercise); changes in personal and social habits (withdrawal, obnoxiousness, etc.); bipolar, multiple personality, and depressive disorders.

A bridge whose beams are formed from concrete must be reinforced with steel rods, which give the span the flexibility it needs to withstand varying weights and temperatures. In a similar fashion your mind and body have greater ability to withstand pressure with fewer debilitating effects on them if you bring to the problem a disciplined mind and a disciplined body. These elements give them a measure of endurance.

A disciplined mind approaches pressures with purpose and structure. For example, a college student with a well-ordered mind can absorb the unexpected demands of additional academic or job assignments without too much ill effect. He merely reprioritizes his responsibilities, adjusts his schedule and his mindset, and meets the challenges with minimal upset.

Others, however, who are already dropping the ball because they live from minute to minute putting out whatever brushfire looms the biggest before them, do not handle unexpected demands well. They panic, push back, lash out, shift blame, or give up. They lack the mental structure and purpose to absorb the unexpected.

Similarly, a disciplined body will be healthier because it receives adequate and consistent amounts of nutrition, rest, and exercise and can therefore meet unexpected demands better than a body whose autoimmune system is compromised because of fatigue, disease, malnutrition, or lack of exercise.

It is crucial to understand, however, that God never intended man to be able to handle the pressures of life on his own. This is true even if his mind and body are disciplined to the highest possible human level. Notice God's thoughts on this:

> Man shall not live by bread alone, but by every word that proceedeth out of the mouth of God. (Matthew 4:4)

> Abide in me, and I in you. As the branch cannot bear fruit of itself, except it abide in the vine; no more can ye, except ye abide in me . . . for without me ye can do nothing. (John 15:4–5)

> Not that we are sufficient of ourselves to think any thing as of ourselves; but our sufficiency is of God. (2 Corinthians 3:5)

> But we have this treasure in earthen vessels, that the excellency of the power may be of God, and not of us. (2 Corinthians 4:7)

Discipline of mind and body alone are very helpful but never enough to handle life's demands adequately. The passages above—and many others in the Scriptures—remind us that we need God. The sagging beams in figure 1 illustrate this truth.

Most people do not adequately discipline their bodies, however, and are also quite selective of the areas of life in which they maintain disciplined mental processes. In addition, they face extra pressures such as fear, anger, and unresolved guilt in areas of responsibility where they have failed God and others.

They are aware that their lives, while productive in some areas, do not effectively honor the Lord. The result is a pathetic picture like figure 2.

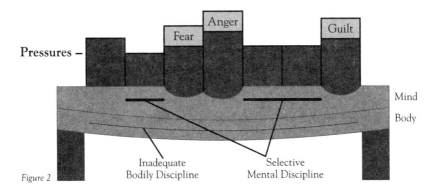

Figure 2

Consider that each box on the bridge is an area of responsibility. The first one may represent your marriage and the second your work. Think of the third as a position you hold in your church—with a weight of fear upon it because you are unsure about your competence to lead in that responsibility. The fourth box is the responsibility you have for the rearing of your children. Right now the relationships with your children is strained, and you bear the weight of unresolved anger as well. The fifth box is some hobby you have picked up and the sixth is the care of your home and lawn. The final responsibility is your relationship with your in-laws and other relationships. Since you have not handled those well, a burden of guilt adds extra pressure to that responsibility.

Notice that under the second box—your work—and under the fifth and sixth boxes—your hobby and your home—there is a small segment of reinforcing bar—selective mental discipline. That mental discipline in those areas exists because you enjoy these responsibilities and apply yourself diligently to them.

Unfortunately, none of us has the luxury of facing only one pressure at a time. Nor do we handle those responsibilities equally well. Our lives reflect to some degree the picture in figure 2.

HANDLING PRESSURE BIBLICALLY

We must ask ourselves, "Where do we start in changing the nature of this picture? How can we make the changes we need to make to have a quiet soul amidst all the pressures of life?"

First, we must eliminate the pressures God does not intend for us to bear. The first of those is sin and its results. There is nothing that God intends to pressure us more than the guilt of our sin. He has designed guilt to weigh heavily upon our souls—so heavily that we cannot ignore it. He wants to reestablish fellowship with us, and that requires that we confess our sins and accept His forgiveness. Listen to John's teaching in this regard.

> If we confess our sins, he is faithful and just to forgive us our sins, and to cleanse us from all unrighteousness. (1 John 1:9)

This is what Isaiah is referring to when he tells us,

> Seek ye the Lord while he may be found, call ye upon him while he is near: let the wicked forsake his way, and the unrighteous man his thoughts: and let him return unto the Lord, and he will have mercy upon him; and to our God, for he will abundantly pardon. (Isaiah 55:6–7)

> Behold, the Lord's hand is not shortened, that it cannot save; neither his ear heavy, that it cannot hear: but your iniquities have separated between you and your God, and your sins have hid his face from you, that he will not hear. (Isaiah 59:1–2)

It is useless for us to restructure and simplify our lives in order to find peace of mind when we are covering sin. Sin must be confessed and forsaken (Proverbs 28:13). We cannot coddle ourselves on this matter and justify our unbelief, deception, impatience, worry, hatred, bitterness, sexual impurity, gossip, and other forms of self-centered behaviors and attitudes. We must see our sin as God sees it, confess it, and accept His forgiveness. It is only then that the enormous burden of sin is lifted from our minds. There can be no lasting peace while we cover sin.

Then we must eliminate responsibilities we have assumed outside the will of God for us. We can easily fill our lives with good things that are motivated by self-centered desires. John informs us:

> The lust of the flesh [inordinate desire for pleasure], and the lust of the eyes [inordinate desire for possessions], and the pride of life [inordinate desire for power and prestige], is not of the Father, but is of the world. (1 John 2:16)

We likely have added activities and responsibilities to our schedule, which in themselves may be fine but may not be what the Lord has for us now. For example, we can take on the chairmanship of a church homeschooling committee out of desire to be acknowledged by others— the pride of life. We can obsessively attempt to keep up with all the messages on our social networking account because we do not want anyone to think ill of us—the pride of life again. We can assume responsibility for an after-school soccer league for the same reason. We can add a part-time job because we want to have material possessions that will make others think well of us—lust of the eyes—and so forth.

We must be brutally honest with ourselves about why we are doing what we are doing. If we are feeding our lusts by our pursuits, we must repent of pursuing them and then look for ways to eliminate them from our schedules if they, indeed, are not the will of God for us.

Be cautious, however. There may be some things we should be doing, but our motives are still corrupt. Perhaps we should chair the home-school committee or assist with the soccer league. In those cases, we need to confess our self-serving motives and do the will of God from a pure heart (1 Timothy 1:5).

I feel especially burdened for what many parents are doing to their children these days by overloading them with a full schedule of after-school activities and allowing them to pursue an unending diet of video and computer games. Not only is the constant push harmful to their bodies, but it is impossible to effectively parent from the driver's seat of a minivan. Others have written extensively on this subject so I won't pursue it further here, but I see the physical and spiritual effects of this sort of harried upbringing when the child gets to college, and I am concerned.

Oftentimes it is not easy in the milieu of our lives to discern these matters. We will need to pull back for some extended time with God in His Word, asking Him to show us our hearts (Psalm 139:23–24). We might also need to seek the counsel of someone who knows us well—perhaps our spouse or a parent—or someone who knows the Scriptures well (Romans 15:14) and can give wise counsel.

Secondly, we must reinforce the beams so they will withstand the weight of the pressures we bear in the will of God. Again, notice the reinforcing bars of discipline in the beams. They remind us that a disciplined body is helpful. We need adequate rest, a nutritious diet, and regular exercise. These are often neglected by God's people today. As a consequence their autoimmune system is compromised, and they are losing the battle against disease. They are often fatigued, and subsequently, ill-tempered, and they gain unnecessary weight with its enormous ramifications for decreased bodily function. These physical debilitations, which can often—though not always—be minimized by personal discipline, add significant pressures to life.

The same is true for mental discipline as we saw earlier in this chapter. But even a disciplined mind is not enough. A *renewed mind*, however, is essential. We must learn to filter everything we think through a biblical grid that allows us to see life as God sees it. We must increase what we know to be true about God and His ways.

The following are the thoughts—and often the verbal expressions—of a person without a renewed mind. He is looking at life through his own eyes only, not those of the Lord.

- "That's one more crummy thing I have to do. I'll never make it!"

- "I think this requirement is stupid, but if that's the only way I can get what I want, I'll do it."

- "This kind of stuff always happens to me! Doesn't anybody care?"

I'm sure you can see how ludicrous it would be to imagine Christ think-ing this way about the pressures that came His way while on the earth. He didn't get upset that another leper or another blind person crossed His path begging for help. He didn't protect His agenda from God's agenda. He came to do the Father's will—not His own.

If things are going to change for us, the change must be in the way we think about life, ourselves, God, and a multitude of other things. Paul made it clear to us that biblical change takes place in the *mind*. He says that we are "transformed by the renewing of [our] mind" (Romans 12:2). Let's see what that looks like and what effect it has upon the way we handle the challenges of life.

A DIFFERENT WAY OF LOOKING AT LIFE AND ITS PRESSURES

A renewed mind possesses a Bible-taught and Spirit-illuminated belief that God is more than enough for everything we need in life. A renewed mind provides the stability needed to hold up under the pressures of life. Fig-ure 3 illustrates the fact that how much something stresses us is entirely a matter of perception based upon our current set of beliefs about our life and about God.

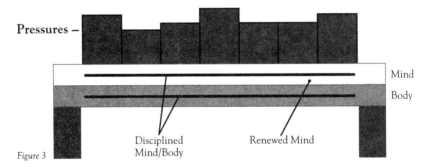

Figure 3

A Christian who knows God well and is doing the will of God has a wonderful "overdraft protection" in what he knows to be true about God. How "stressed" he feels has everything to do with what is going on in his mind. This kind of renewed mind requires structured satura-tion—something we'll discuss in the final chapter of this book.

It is not enough to take a Pollyanna approach to life's challenges and merely try to find the *good* in every situation. A renewed mind sees *God* in every situation and thus responds to the challenges in a way that honors God and brings stability to life.

If we are to have a renewed mind, however, we must spend much time beholding God in His Word. The chapters in part two of this book will target key areas of God's nature that you must understand and believe if you are to have a quiet soul.

FOR YOUR ENCOURAGEMENT

I want to close this chapter with three brief testimonies of people who have used the *Quieting a Noisy Soul Counseling Program* to address their long-standing problems. They have found the wonderful difference that a renewed mind makes—a mind that believes what God has said and a heart that fellowships with God Himself. My prayer is that you will have such a testimony in the days ahead as you allow God to address your noisy soul with His Word.

From Kathy

"My family gave me the *Quieting a Noisy Soul Counseling Program* for Christmas last year. God has taught me so much through it. I have battled depression since I was 18, along with an eating disorder. I was saved at age 27.

"I first sought help from medical doctors for the depression. I was told I had a hereditary chemical imbalance that would require lifelong treatment with medication in the same way that a diabetic must take insulin for his condition.

"This sent me down a path of wrong thinking that lasted for 14 years. In my mind, my problem was not sin, but a physical condition. Thankfully, God is gracious and merciful. I now know and believe the truth concerning the root cause of depression and anxiety. I also know and believe the truth about the Source of my peace and joy—Jesus Christ.

"Trying to get off the medication after 14 years was an unbelievable battle, but Christ gave the victory. I hate to see other Christians go down this wrong path since more and more are experiencing these problems, and it is more and more common for doctors to prescribe medication as the answer. It hasn't been easy, but I can testify to God's victory in my life in the area of depression and the eating disorder. I am continuing to learn that God is good and that He is enough. Of course I have to remind myself that daily! I have been able to help so many people through what I have learned in this counseling program."

From Cyndi

"I was introduced to *Quieting a Noisy Soul* last year through the recommendation of my pastor's wife who I was meeting with for counseling. I was struggling with fear, anxiety, and panic attacks, which I believed were the result of having been sexually abused for 9 years as a child. I had gone to therapy, counseling, and even 'Christian' counseling for over 20 years and had quite frankly lost hope that I could overcome my past.

"The biblical counseling I received from my pastor's wife provided a flicker of hope and encouraged me to approach this series with an open mind. Having been in worldly counseling for so long, I had been focusing on my emotions/feelings and they were running my life. I think the truth that made the most difference to me was discovering that my thoughts drove my emotions and not the other way around. That was an amazing concept for me. As I learned to track my thoughts, I began to see biblical change like I had never seen it before. God through this study has been an amazing journey, and I am so grateful to the Lord for revealing His truth to me through this study.

"The Lord is now using me to counsel other ladies from the women's shelter that is through our church. I cannot tell you how grateful I am to the Lord that He is able to use me in spite of my past."

From Liz

Liz's marriage was in trouble. She had isolated her adult children through her controlling ways, was more than one hundred pounds overweight, had sleep problems, was failing at work, and was very depressed. She began working through these principles and within four short months was on her way back to a vibrant walk with God. She has much ground yet to cover but has made much progress. She told me the following when I asked what she would tell someone else who had similar problems.

"If someone came to me with similar problems that I have had, I believe I would have to direct them to seeing God is not in their picture. Although I had heard many messages, prayed, spent much time with God, and at times had glimpses of this wonderful walk, it never lasted long enough to really be alive to me.

"I did not see that my discontent was actually unbelief in the God Who loves me. God broke my heart about this and showed me my sinfulness. This was first and foremost.

"I was so self-focused; I saw nothing else. I had to repent first of my sin of discontent. I had to relinquish control of what I thought worked to the One Who works all things for my good.

"I am learning that He is the One in control. I am learning that He gives peace that I cannot conjure up on my own. I used to live a life of trying to 'do' right without any repentance. It didn't work.

"Before I did not read my Bible except on occasion. I did not think on truths I had heard or learned in church or in a message. Today I ponder them, think on them, and try to learn more so that I can know this God that I have barely known before. The God I knew then was heavy-handed and was ready to pounce on me at any time. The God I am beginning to know loves me, is kind to me, and continually shows me new things.

"Sorrow never drove me to Him before; it drove me to despair. Frustration ran deep. I felt unstable most of the time and worried constantly. I lived a life of what if's and questioned everything.

"I tried to live the Christian life without God in the picture. Now I talk to Him, and He talks back in His Word. When I read the Word, it becomes real to me, and God 'turns the lights on' in a way I never knew before.

"God has even changed my disposition towards the people I work with—the people who hurt me. Even Christmas is different for me this year. I'm not super-materialistic, but I usually have a few things in mind for Christmas and used to focus on what I could get.

"I couldn't think of anything I wanted this year—really. The only things I could think of were books or recorded messages or something to help me grow. The message 'God Is More than Enough' [from *Quieting a Noisy Soul*] was the beginning of a new life for me."

What I want you to see from these brief scenarios is that God is perfectly able to quiet our souls as we meditate upon His Word. Appendix B has two more, and extended, encouraging testimonies about Jennie and Anne. These stories can be duplicated by the hundreds. "Grace and peace" is, indeed, "multiplied unto you through the knowledge of God" (2 Peter 1:2). May it be true of you as well as you meditate upon these truths.

In the next two chapters we will discover what these women learned about their spiritual lives. They were on "The Way Down" to anxiety, anger, and despair. Once they knew how they got were they were, they were ready to learn "The Way Back."

Take Time to Reflect

1. This chapter listed several physical and emotional effects of wrongly handled pressure. List the ones that are true of you.

2. In order for you to have the renewed mind that comes by seeing the things that are invisible and eternal, you must spend much time each day with God. No one is truly stable without *taking time* to get God's perspective of life and, more importantly, to see God Himself. According to what God says is true in 2 Corinthians 4:16–18, what will need to change in your schedule if you are to have your "inward man"—your spirit—renewed and encouraged every day in the midst of pressures?

Chapter Four

TRACKING "THE WAY DOWN," PART 1

When they knew God, they glorified him not as God, neither were thankful; but became vain in their imaginations, and their foolish heart was darkened. (Romans 1:21)

We have laid a foundation for some very important concepts for our Christian growth in Christlikeness and for the resulting stability and testimony of our lives. I want to begin with an overview of some additional concepts that will be more fully developed later. I call this overview "The Way Down" because it describes the disintegration of the human soul when it operates in unbelief.

As you see in the diagram on page 35, though it is shaped somewhat like a baseball diamond with an additional position in center field, the flow of action does not follow the flow of baseball around the bases. In "The Way Down" chart the flow starts with Unbelief (center field), moves to Discontent (second base), then to Anxiety (third base) and/or Anger (first base), and, ultimately, ends in Despair (home plate). The pathway down is both predictable and preventable. It is crucial that you understand this if you are to deal with the noise in your own soul and if you are to be used of God to help others with noisy souls. Take a few minutes to study the chart.

UNBELIEF—"THE GREAT DISORDER" OF THE HEART

Unbelief is a "dis-order" because it places things in the wrong *order*. It accepts the reasonings of man—his vain imaginations—over the revelation of God.

Unbelief

The "Great Disorder"
of the heart

The Lie of Unbelief: "God is
not doing enough for me; God
Himself is not enough for me.
I need something more."

Discontent

A "lust for more" is the basis
for every temptation in the heart

"If only I had what I need."
"I should be/have…"
"I don't like…"

Anxiety

The emotion of uncertainty

"What if I don't get what I need?"

Anger

The emotion of displeasure

"I'm upset because I don't
have what I need."

Despair

The emotion of hopelessness

"I'll never get what I need."

For example, God very clearly says that He loves us (Jeremiah 31:3), yet a Christian can respond, "Yes, but He doesn't love *me*!" He rejects God's truth—which is unbelief—and elevates his own conclusions above God's. The conclusions he has drawn are lies. God cannot love everyone and not love me.

As Romans 1:23 says, man left to himself exchanges the truth of God for a lie. Notice God's concern about this in Isaiah 55:7–9.

> Let the wicked forsake his way, and the unrighteous man his thoughts: and let him return unto the Lord, and he will have mercy upon him; and to our God, for he will abundantly pardon. For my thoughts are not your thoughts, neither are your ways my ways, saith the Lord. For as the heavens are higher than the earth, so are my ways higher than your ways, and my thoughts than your thoughts.

Here is the tension. Will we choose to lend more weight to God's thoughts, or will we give greater weight to our thoughts about life and how it is to be lived? We must ask ourselves, "Is it really true that God has spoken? Does He care about us? Will He do what He says He will do? Is sin as bad as He says it is? Is there really forgiveness for any sin? Does He really answer prayer? Is holiness as important as He says it is? Will I, indeed, reap what I sow?"

Remember that rejecting any of these things that God says are true is to be guilty of unbelief. Unbelief is a harder sin to recognize than lying, anger, bitterness, laziness, adultery, or profanity. It hides in the shadows of our soul. Only the light of God's truth—the Bible—can expose the unbelief of our hearts.

We must see unbelief as the mother sin—it gives birth to all the others. We are so blinded by our unbelief, however, that we cannot see how it can possibly have anything to do with our present misery and the noise in our souls.

We think our problem is that we are experiencing panic attacks, or bitterness over our mistreatment or abuse, or fear because of the unpredictable authorities in our lives, or anger because an important person to us walked out of our life, or anorexia because we are too fat. These are symptoms; they are not the problem. You will be able to see by the end of our study together that at the root of all of these sins—and many others—is unbelief.

Please don't let that last statement trouble you. It should give you much hope! There is divine remedy for unbelief! The guilt in our heart and the resulting noise in our souls can be removed.

As we shall see as we go along, most of the psychiatric "disorders" of our day are rooted in "The Great Disorder" of unbelief in the heart. It should be no surprise to us that these psychiatric disorders are increasing when their root cause—the rejection of truth by the world and the forgetfulness and ignorance of truth by God's people—is more prevalent.

God has promised that unbelief will lead to disintegration as we have seen from Romans 1. We should not be surprised—though we should be grieved—to see what is happening around us today. The unbelieving world increasingly rejects the truth about God, while the believing world increasingly ignores the truth about God. The result will be the same disintegration for both groups. We must see all of life through God's eyes—through the lens of the Scriptures.

I want you to consider several passages of Scripture to see how different our modern view of problems is when compared to God's view. Our thoughts, indeed, are not His thoughts (Isaiah 55:7–9).

In Numbers 20:1–13 Moses was upset with the children of Israel because again they were complaining and challenging his leadership. Moses in anger struck the rock in disobedience to God's command to speak to the rock. Notice that God did not correct and chasten Moses for anger when he struck the rock. God charged both him and Aaron with unbelief (20:12). God makes a divine connection that says the *root of anger is unbelief.* Someone is not seeing God in the picture. He is seeing only the problem before him and the desires of his own heart to have something on his own terms.

When the disciples were panic stricken by a storm, Jesus' comment to them revealed that the *root of fear is unbelief* (Mark 4:40). We tend to excuse their terror as a natural fear when facing the elements. But Jesus is present with us in our storms and to charge Him with being uncaring is unbelief.

The writer of Hebrews teaches that the *root of despair is unbelief* when he cautions his readers to run the Christian race with endurance by looking to the Jesus, the One Who began our spiritual life and will bring it to completion (Hebrews 12:1–3). He warns that if we do not think on the work and example of Christ on our behalf we will become weary and will faint in our minds. Wrong thinking leads to wrong emotions—discouragement and despair—and wrong thinking consequently leads to giving up.

At the root of "The Great Disorder" of unbelief is a lie—a fantasy. It is the lie that "God is not doing enough for me; God Himself is not enough for me. I need something more."

Sometimes people who do not know God well have a hard time imagining that God can be enough for them in their trials. They question how a person can be all that we need when there are bills to pay, children to feed and clothe, work responsibilities to fulfill, and all of that under the pressures of ill-health, financial setbacks, and relational conflicts.

Those of us who are married have tasted that concept, however. Before Patty and I were married, we would look at our bank account—which had only a few hundred dollars in it—and we knew that the wedding would be very simple, our rental apartment very small and sparsely furnished, and our car fairly unpredictable because I still faced one more year of college.

Still, in spite of our very meager possessions and somewhat frightening economic situation when we considered the expenses of the upcoming wedding and of setting up housekeeping, all that seemed to matter very little because we had each other. I remember thinking, "We don't need much furniture, and we don't have to eat fancy meals; we can eat lots of macaroni and cheese" (and we did!). The point is that we found our happiness and contentedness in a relationship, not in our circumstances.

The same principle applies but on a much grander scale when we know God well and consider the kind of person Who is in our circumstances with us. This was the attitude of the prophets and apostles. Though they faced persecution and adversity, they were amazingly joyful and content because of what they experienced in their relationship with God Himself. This is the divine intention for all of us.

We must learn to interpret our experiences by what we know about God through His Word instead of interpreting what God is like by our experiences. If we do not ground our belief about the nature of God and His disposition to us in the Scriptures, we will reject much of what He says about Himself when we face difficulty.

If we reject what God says to be true about Himself and about the way things work in His world, all we are left with is a fantasy—a world of our imagination about Who He is and how His world works. The seriousness of this fantasy is that it is a break with reality. Consider carefully these statements.

A world where God does not love us does not exist. If you think you live in a world where God does not love you, you have chosen to live in a fantasy world. You are experiencing a break with reality because of your unbelief—your rejection of what is true about God. The same divine logic applies to the following statements.

A world where God is not in control of all things for our good and His glory does not exist.

A world where God is not with me or where He does not hear my cry does not exist.

A world where God is heavy-handed and mean-spirited and where He is just waiting for us to mess up so that He can club us does not exist.

These are fantasy worlds of our imagination. They are not real worlds. They do not exist. Therefore, trying to live in them with these beliefs does not work well. It would be like trying to live in a world where you believed up was down and down was up. You would always be frustrated at how things were working out for you.

Philippians 4:19 describes one aspect of the "real world." Paul says, "But my God shall supply all your need according to his riches in glory by Christ Jesus." Reality, according to this passage, is that God is enough for me. He will supply all I really need. If He doesn't supply the possessions or health we think we need, He will supply us with the grace we need to be content. We can find Him to be "more than enough" for us. I'll have more to say about this in chapter 6.

DISCONTENT

Unbelief truly hides in the shadows of our thoughts, does it not? It is hard to see our unbelief most of the time. Discontent (second base) is somewhat easier to recognize and flows out of the unbelief (center field) that we have been discussing.

Discontent is the dissatisfaction of not having what we have decided in our unbelief that we must have in order for life to work. No one can be thoroughly content with God and what God has provided and still be anxious, angry, or depressed that he doesn't have something he needs. Our discontent, which is rooted in unbelief as we have seen, is at the root of all these.

The whining of our discontented hearts is familiar to us. It is often accompanied by "if only" thoughts, and often expressions, like these.

"*If only* my spouse/boss/parents would try to understand me."

"*If only* people appreciated me more."

"*If only* I had more freedom/more money/more say."

"*If only* I had better health/less pain/fewer doctor bills/more answers."

"*If only* I had not messed up/had not been abused/had not gotten drunk."

"*If only* I had grown up with different parents/different brothers and sisters."

"*If only* I were married/were single again/were married to someone who loves me."

"*If only* I had finished college/had answered the call to preach years ago/had not run away."

All these imply that the one thinking these things lacks something he must have in order to be content in his present situation. Each of these situations naturally involves a loss. The sorrow over that loss can eventually lead to despair, as we shall see in the next chapter.

For now, I want you to see how easily we can begin tracking our discontented thoughts by watching for "if only" patterns. But there are two more tell-tale thought patterns that reveal discontented thinking. The second is "I should be/have . . ." thoughts. Remember, we must become skilled at tracking our thinking, not our feelings.

"By now *I should be* rich/married/through with college/successful."

"By now *I should have* a higher paying job/a family that respects me/a debt-free financial picture/a decent home."

One more indication of discontent is "I don't like . . ." thoughts.

"*I don't like* my circumstances/my job/my spouse/my standard of living."

"*I don't like* having to depend upon other people for help."

"*I don't like* it that my body won't let me work like I used to work."

"*I don't like* having to work so hard when life is easier for others."

"*I don't like* it when I work hard and nobody seems to notice."

All these thoughts are dangerous because "a lust for more" is the basis for every temptation in the heart according to James 1:14:

> Every man is tempted, when he is drawn away of his own lust, and enticed.

James teaches us that once we have decided that we really must have something, we are "sitting ducks" for a temptation that will lead us into sin. We cannot be tempted with something unless we really want it. These strong desires (lusts) to have something some other way will provide the point of contact within your soul from which temptation will breed sinful actions and other sinful attitudes.

This kind of thinking was at the heart of the sins of the children of Israel in the wilderness (Numbers 11–16).

"*If only* life were easier in this wilderness."

"*If only* we had water and something besides this manna."

"*If only* we had more say; Moses takes on too much authority for himself."

"*If only* we were back in Egypt."

"*If only* we were dead like our brothers who died in the wilderness."

This line of thinking is absolutely toxic to Christlikeness! Begin a list of your own "if onlys," "I shoulds," and "I don't likes." These are the precancer cells of the soul. Left unattended they will destroy you.

We of all people—who have the truth about God—ought to be the most joyful, thankful, and contented people! Of course, we have our challenges and setbacks, but legitimate concerns should be turned into prayer requests and brought before God while surrendering the results to God. We must reject the lies and hold onto what we know to be true about God. Otherwise, the lie of unbelief will take on the form of discontent and will drive the inevitable anxiety, anger, and despair to follow.

Learn to look for the roots of unbelief and discontent when the fruits of guilt, anxiety, anger, and despair bud on the branches of your heart.

Take Time to Reflect

1. Why do we call unbelief "The Great Disorder of the Heart?"

2. What parallel is there between the phrase "neither were they thankful" in Romans 1:21 and the "discontent" seen on the chart?

3. Hebrews 3:7–19 speaks about why the children of Israel did not enter into a land of rest but wandered in the wilderness for forty years. What does this passage teach about the connection between unbelief and unrest?

Chapter Five

TRACKING "THE WAY DOWN," PART 2

When they knew God, they glorified him not as God, neither were thankful; but became vain in their imaginations, and their foolish heart was darkened. (Romans 1:21)

God has made unbelief a serious issue in the Bible. Spiritual problems of unbelief are not limited to outward ways of making life work without God: lying, materialism, immorality, gossip, and so forth. Unbelief manifests itself in many behind the scenes ways as well: discontent, guilt, anxiety, anger, and despair.

In the last chapter we looked at "The Great Disorder" of unbelief and noticed how it first manifests itself in discontent—the lie that we have to have something more for our lives to be joy-filled and peace-full. We want in this chapter to move on down "The Way Down" chart and look at the next manifestations of our unbelief—anxiety, anger, and despair. Look back at the chart on page 35 to orient yourself to these indications of unbelief.

ANXIETY

Anxiety is a subset of fear—*the emotion of uncertainty*. It is an emotion of vulnerability. For simplification I will use the words *anxiety*, *fear*, and *worry* synonymously in our discussion here.

We saw that discontent shows up in "if only" thinking. Again, *learn to track your thoughts*, not your feelings. Anxiety manifests itself in "what if" thinking like these.

> "*What if* the plant shuts down/the boss isn't happy with my work/I don't get the raise?"

"*What if* my husband is into pornography/my teenager is doing drugs/my wife is interested in another man?"

"*What if* I get up to sing a solo in church and my voice gives out/I trip going up the steps to the platform?"

"*What if* I get sick in front of all those people/I go crazy in public?"

"What if this headache is really from a brain tumor/I have an incurable disease?"

"*What if* I have another panic attack, but this time while I'm driving?"

"*What if* I can't sleep again tonight?"

"*What if* someone breaks into the house and kills all of us/kills everyone but me?"

"*What if* no one at the church potluck dinner chooses my casserole?"

"*What if* I'm the only one at the meeting wearing a suit and tie/wearing a dress/wearing pants?"

On and on it goes. The worrier can take any situation and imagine multiple scenarios of how things can go wrong. And while they spend much time imagining the future, God is never a part of the future situations they dwell on.

Worriers meditate upon possibilities.

They focus on uncertainties instead of meditating upon certainties of what they know to be true about God from the Scriptures and what He has promised to His people.

The thinking of anxious people is often catastrophic, negative, over-reactive, and unrestrained. Their belief says that they need something more to be content, and now they are afraid they will not get it. They fill their thinking with the uncertainties that can destroy what they have decided they must have.

Worriers often meditate upon impossibilities.

Perfectionistic people, at heart, are usually great worriers. They want everything to go just right because they know what they think they must have to make life work. They must do everything right so that everything will turn out right for them. They often think they must be the right weight, have the right image, have the perfect devotional life, always perform at peak, never make any mistakes, never be vulnerable, and never show any flaws, weaknesses, or sins. Consequently, their lives become very intense, and their souls are very noisy.

In the financial realm it takes an enormous amount of money to be self-insured. Perfectionistic people generally attempt to be "self-insured." They must accumulate much knowledge and control, but it is never enough. Consequently, they are left feeling quite vulnerable—fearful. They are not trusting their underwriter.

Worriers scare themselves with their imaginations and fantasies.

Like the child who convinces himself that a monster is lurking under his bed or in the closet, a worrier creates his own monsters and produces his own panic. We will see a thread running through the issues of anxiety, anger, and despair as we watch them unfold in this book. We cannot eat mental roadkill and have healthy souls. We must learn to think biblically about every situation in life.

Worriers are masters at meditation.

They know how to take one thought and examine it from every possible angle. They know how to carry that thought with them throughout the day. It presses into their consciousness whenever something else isn't occupying their attention. They know how to take that one thought and apply it to every part of life. They are so intent upon making sure that what they have decided they must have is not spoiled by anything. They are on a quest to make sure that nothing goes wrong, so they must be prepared for every unexpected turn in the road.

Worry is the root cause of what the world calls the "psychological anxiety disorders" today—including panic attacks, obsessive thinking, compulsive behavior, anorexia, bulimia, generalized anxiety, and phobias. The world doesn't offer the right solutions to these problems, ultimately, because they leave God out of even helpful strategies, but the world has rightly called them anxiety disorders. God is not in the proper place. Life is *out of order*.

Worry is also the root cause of many physical problems and aggravates others. To understand this we must learn what happens to our autonomic nervous system (ANS) when we worry. The portion of the ANS called the sympathetic nervous system produces our "fight or flight" stress response when we encounter an emergency of some sort. When our mind registers a danger, many processes are activated. For example, the adrenal glands produce adrenalin, which quickens the heart rate, raises the blood sugar for muscle activity, dilates the pupils, stops digestion, and speeds up breathing to get the body ready to face the danger. (This process is described in much greater detail in several articles listed in the quickstart section of QuietingaNoisySoul.com.)

If you are driving down a two-lane country road and notice a truck coming at you in your lane as the driver tries to pass an oncoming car, your *mind* immediately registers the emergency. If something isn't done quickly, you will become his hood ornament. Instantly the sympathetic nervous system gets you ready for action, as described above. You instinctively pull your car off to the shoulder while the truck passes in your lane. As you stop your car alongside the road to recover a bit, your chest heaves, your hands are clammy, your muscles are tense, and your heart races as if you had just finished a strenuous footrace. Yet you have not exerted yourself physically at all. Every one of these bodily changes come about by your *mind* concluding that you were in danger. Even after a few minutes sitting in your car, you are still jumpy from the adrenalin.

What is interesting is that you can experience many of these same physical manifestations as you rethink the episode or as you tell it to someone later. This happens because the sympathetic nervous system does not distinguish between a real emergency—your incident with the truck on the road—and an imaginary emergency—your retelling or rethinking the incident.

Worriers create imaginary emergencies in their mind.

By imaginary I mean that the emergency is not happening at that moment, though it may, indeed, be possible sometime in the future—or may have happened in the past. Thus, the worrier keeps his body on high alert. Eventually, he will begin to experience negative effects in his body—gastrointestinal problems, endocrine gland fatigue, chronic pain, high blood pressure and other cardio difficulties, headaches from muscular tension, weight gain, insomnia, and so forth.

His body reacts very much like his car would if he sat in his car in the garage, started the engine, and held the accelerator to the floor while parked in neutral with the emergency brake on. Depending upon the condition of the car, he would be able to continue this for only a limited time. Something would eventually melt down. Any number of things could happen: a water hose would break, a bearing would seize, a gasket would blow, or the engine would overheat and the block would crack. The reason for the breakdown is that the energy produced by the engine is designed to be translated into motion, not heat.

In a similar fashion, adrenalin—and other biochemicals—generated during an emergency were designed to get the body ready for real physical danger and are used up confronting that physical danger. In days gone by, a pioneer settler trying to put out a fire in his barn would use up the adrenalin fighting the fire.

A worrier, since he is not using up the energy fighting physical danger, only accumulates the biochemicals that have negative effects upon his bodily systems. This is one reason he must develop a renewed mind so that he thinks about his life's challenges from God's perspective. It is also why a regular noncompetitive program of exercise is so important in today's world since it uses up adrenalin. As I said earlier, *adrenalin is a wonderful friend in a real emergency but a deadly foe as a way of life.*

Consider another factor here. The world of psychiatry says anxiety disorders run in families. We don't deny that these phenomena occur in families, but the cause isn't genetic. Think of it this way. If you speak English, chances are your parents do as well, yet we do not go looking for a genetic marker for native languages. Rather, we acknowledge that families exert powerful influences over every area of a child's life.

We learn what is important and what is not from our families. We learn how to solve problems from our families—or we learn not to solve problems. If mom is deathly afraid of thunderstorms and lightning and panics at the first clap of thunder, one or more of the children are going to become very nervous around thunderstorms. Mom demonstrates by her reactions not only what is dangerous but how to deal with it. She also communicates that worry is acceptable, though God calls it sin.

In a similar fashion, if mom always obsesses about her looks, always trying to take off a few pounds, always trying to wear just the right combination of clothes, and makes offhanded remarks to her junior high daughter about her pudginess, guess who is going to obsess about her body image?

It is true that none of us *needs* our parent's influence to think wrongly about life, but parents who are not thinking biblically about life will make it easier for a child to react with sinful worry to the challenges of life.

I am especially concerned as I see anxiety disorders—and their negative effects upon the body—showing up in children at younger and younger ages. The responsibility must lie at the feet of the adults in their lives who do not model biblical problem solving, who keep their little bodies on an adrenalin high alert by cramming their schedules with more and more activities, who allow the children to experience more and more frightening and intense situations through entertainment choices— movies, television, perpetual electronic communication, and electronic gaming, or who have unresolved family conflicts themselves.

Anxiety is the fear that I will not get what I need or want. It is driven by unbelief and discontent. This is why anxiety is always portrayed in the Bible as a spiritual problem: "God is not doing enough for me; God Himself is not enough for me. I need something more, and I'm afraid I won't get it." We will not be anxious if we know God well and are content with what He has provided because we have found Him to be more than enough for us.[1]

If those last words seem too simplistic to you and/or do not generate any hope in your soul, stay with me. The purpose of this book—especially in part two—is to show you how that is possible.

ANGER

Anger is a strong emotion of displeasure. It says, "I don't like what is going on," or "I don't have what I need, and I'm upset."

Generally, our anger reveals another area of our lives that is not surrendered to God. It is noteworthy that most people whose lives are characterized by anger are also self-centered. That doesn't necessarily mean that they arrogantly think life should revolve around them—though for some that is exactly the problem. Pain, frustration, and fear—the main causes of anger—tend to lead us to focus on ourselves and what is happening to us. The result is a self-centered perspective of life.

People express their anger often in destructive ways—cutting words, violent actions, relational conflict, and sometimes self-injury. Though we cannot unpack all the dynamics of anger in this chapter, please note its place on "The Way Down" chart and try to understand its essential nature of displeasure.[2] Again, however, we will not be angry if we know God well and are content with what He has provided because we have found Him to be more than enough for us.

DESPAIR

Lastly, notice that anxiety and anger lead eventually to despair—the emotion of hopelessness. The one fearing that he won't get what he thinks he needs or angry that he isn't getting what he thinks he needs will eventually realize that he will *never* get what he thinks he needs in the way he wants it. It is no surprise then to hear even secular sources say that anxiety and despair often go together. They feed each other.

In addition, we often see today combinations of anger and despair. A person who bounces back and forth between them will often be labeled bipolar. He isn't suffering from supposed chemical imbalances; he is experiencing the unpredictable consequences of living on "the way down."

Despair—what others call psychological depression—exists when a person sorrows about his losses in life without any hope. Those losses can be tangible—losing a friend, spouse, job, valued possession—or intangible—loss of respect in someone's eyes, loss of an opportunity, loss of control in a situation, loss of equilibrium in a relationship. The hopelessness is often laced with self-pity, making the condition more toxic to the person's spiritual state—and, thus, his emotional state.

We need to note in passing that "feeling down" is not sinful and can be caused by bodily conditions. We can feel down from fatigue, disease, hormone levels, lack of exercise, poor nutrition, recent surgery, and so forth. It is crucial to understand, however, that thinking hopeless *thoughts* is entirely a matter of the heart and is an indication of spiritual needs.[3]

We must again note that we will not despair when facing the losses of life if we know God well and are content with what He has provided because we have found Him to be more than enough for us.

From Barbara

We have tracked "The Way Down," which will provide a reference point for our study in the chapters ahead. I want to close this chapter with a couple of testimonies. The first is from Barbara, a Christian school teacher who came to me after her doctor told her that the next step in treating her anxiety and bipolar tendencies was to begin psychiatric medication but warned her that if that didn't work her bipolar tendencies would have to be treated through psychiatric hospitalization. She was seriously dysfunctional. The second is from a pastor who experienced severe panic attacks. They both illustrate how God quiets noisy souls through the work of His Word and His Spirit.

Barbara sent me the following e-mail three months after she began applying the principles taught in the *Quieting a Noisy Soul Counseling Program.*

"This past year, I have been in such a daze—either despairing or depressed or anxious or just plain confused about the direction I was headed. There would be bright spots where I would learn something about God—His love, His faithfulness, His mercy, etc., but it would never stick. I was going in circles and I hated it. Life just didn't have a purpose; it was full of hectic activity and huge letdowns. I never felt stable and at rest. I knew things about God, but I never seemed to be able to make sense of it all. When I would talk to my supervisor at school, I would see the direction I needed to go and more pieces would fall into place, but I still doubted whether I would ever get free of this whole mess.

"After God gave me a good summer and taught me so many lessons about Himself, I was hoping that everything would be okay. But when school started, it seemed that I went deeper into despair and hopelessness than ever before. Something had to give or I was going to end up in the psych hospital. I felt like I was going crazy.

"Even after we talked [the first time], I still did not get it. I was so discouraged. I was so sick of being a fake and trying to pretend that I was at rest or was learning something about God, when I wasn't. And there were so many times in the past that I thought I had finally gotten it—only to be disappointed each time. I was so sick of failure and didn't even think that I would be able to recognize the real thing because I was so sure by this time that I couldn't have a stable relationship with God.

"All of these struggles were affecting every area of my life—I wasn't teaching well; I wasn't relating to people well; I didn't even want to be around anyone because I couldn't hide my misery anymore, and I didn't want them to see it.

"I look back on all that and am amazed what God rescued me from. I don't think I'm going crazy any longer. My soul is quiet, where it was frantic before. I know crucial things about God, not just as facts any longer. Now I am not basing my stability or satisfaction on a passing emotion of joy or peace or hope, but on the never-changing reality of God and all that He is.

"When feelings of uneasiness or anxiety come now, I can look at them through the truth of God and deal with them in a biblical manner. I can truly say that I am free from the power of fear, because when the fears come (and they still do), I know that God is stronger than anything or anyone who can harm me or affect the circumstances around me.

"It's like the hymn verse: "Things that once were wild alarms cannot now disturb my rest; Closed with everlasting arms, Pillowed on the loving breast . . ."

"Even in the face of failure (and I have feared that above all), God is still powerful to forgive, and to give strength in weakness, to carry out His purposes in spite of my human frailty and sin. And when consequences come as the result of sin or circumstances change because of my weakness, God has control of that as well.

"I am sure, as I have never been sure in my life that God loves me, and He wants the best for me, and He will work out everything for His glory and my good.

"I am even to the point where when I see a trial coming or when I am in an impossible situation, I can rejoice because I know that I will learn something else about God and that He will change me more into Christlikeness through it. I always cowered in these situations before and definitely did not have joy or thanksgiving.

"God's timing has been perfect. His plan for me is also perfect. He knew exactly how low He needed to take me, how helpless He needed to make me, and how long He needed this to go on before He showed me things about Himself. I don't think I would have paid sufficient attention if I had not known such a degree of despair. And I would not have learned how to seek for Him with such intensity and, at the same time, such surrender to His timeline and His manner of revealing Himself. He has changed things that I considered strengths into weaknesses so that I had nothing left to offer, nothing left to lean on, nothing left to grab—but Him. And now I want nothing but Him.

"Now that God has gotten truth about Himself through to my stubborn heart, He has already been hard at work in other areas of my life that He would never have been able to touch had He not dealt with me about the control issue.

"I understand now that this process of Christlikeness will go on throughout my life, and I finally see it as a positive thing. Before, I had this sense of drudgery and hopelessness that I would never get it. I couldn't accept the fact that I wasn't perfect. But I know that God loves me just the way I am, that He delights in me now, but that He will continue to work on me because my sin nature continues to get in the way. He doesn't get frustrated with me. He just keeps doing whatever it takes to change me, and that is good for me.

"He has promised that He has the victory in my life and that He will perfect that which concerns me. I can only stand in awe of God's grace and goodness which He is showing me."

Before we leave this chapter, let me share with you Barbara's testimony six years after the original testimony you just read.

"I just thought I'd tell you that as of today I have passed the six year mark of when God let the bottom drop out of my life (or shall I say, He shot my self-sufficient, but disintegrating, planet out of the sky) so that He could begin some intensive rebuilding work in my life.

"He doesn't let me get away with trying to play God anymore. That kind of fantastical nonsense had to stop. I rejoice every day in what He has done, but the anniversary date is a special time for me to marvel that God could rescue even me. It seems like yesterday when I listened to the Scripture Meditations CD for the first time and started going through Isaiah 55. I still remember the quietness of that evening as I wondered what God was going to do with all of that and whether I would feel normal again. I could sense that I was headed for radical change.

"I look back and see a whole bunch of darkness and turmoil and fear swallowed up in light and truth. God continues to make fundamental changes in me and is purifying my life from sin and is stabilizing me in His character and promises. I occasionally still struggle with fear and old thought patterns, but they don't have a stranglehold on me. I know what to do about them when they tempt me. It is still incredible to me to look back and see how things are so different now than they were. The horrible darkness and the feeling of being sucked up into a black hole, and the fear of an imminent meltdown, or of going crazy—It's all gone!

"Only God could do that! God's grace and love and mercy shines brighter for me when I see it against the backdrop of the horrible pit from which He drew me. Even though it has been six years this freedom and hope and peace and rest still feel brand-new and marvelous! I remember and rejoice every chance I get. What a Savior!"

From John

"I began to experience panic attacks five years ago. My first attack came on an airplane in LaGuardia Airport in New York. The plane had begun to taxi, but my panic attack was so severe the pilot returned to the gate.

"The next six months were an incredible journey for me. The answer from the medical community was drugs. I believed that the weapons for the warfare against anxiety were not carnal, and therefore drugs were not an option for me.

"I read and listened to every book and CD that I could get my hands on. No preacher or counselor came to my aid. It was just God and me.

"A friend of mine sent me the counseling program *Quieting a Noisy Soul*, which was my only Bible-based resource. I needed a spiritual solution for my situation, and this was it. I want to thank you for your work in this area. I have used your materials on numerous occasions to help others. In the past six years I have had the opportunity to minister to a great number of men—many in their early 40's—who have run headlong into anxiety and panic.

"I pray that God will continue to use His Truth to defeat the lies of the enemy in the hearts of His people. Thanks again."

Barbara was a young woman with a lifetime mindset of "I must be perfect" and "I must be in control"—filled with anxiety and depression. She was almost nonfunctional and was labeled "manic-depressive" (bipolar) by her physician. She was reluctant to accept the diagnosis and the medication but was motivated to seek help when she realized—as did the doctor—that if something didn't change she would be headed for psychiatric hospitalization. She found that the real answer was "the structured saturation of the Scriptures in a seeking and surrendered heart." I will have much more to say about that later. What she needed to know about God is the subject of our study in the next section: "The Way Back."

Take Time to Reflect

1. You have seen in this session that we need to track our thinking, not our feelings. You have also seen that anxiety shows up in "what if . . ." thinking. List your "what if . . ." thoughts.

2. List your "I don't like . . ." and "I'm upset with . . ." thoughts.

3. List your despairing thoughts of "I'll never get what I need," or "This is hopeless; I may as well give up."

PART TWO

The Way Back

Chapter Six

FINDING THAT GOD
IS MORE THAN ENOUGH

I have learned, in whatsoever state I am, therewith to be content. . . .
I can do all things through Christ which strengtheneth me. (Philippians
4:11, 13)

In December 1998 I began experiencing chest pains at age forty-six. I was especially concerned because my father had died of a heart attack only ten months earlier after quadruple bypass surgery in his fifties followed by several minor strokes some years later.

I had just finished writing *Changed into His Image* and during the process of study for the book felt at times like David on a hillside basking in the amazing glories of our great God! Now I felt like David alone in a valley staring at a nine-foot giant with only a slingshot in my hand.

God gave me a quiet soul as I meditated in His Word and pondered the future possibilities, and I found God to be more than enough for me. After open heart bypass surgery I had twelve weeks of recovery, which I spent studying, meditating, and resting. I specifically studied the topic of contentment. This recovery time was one of the most spiritually satisfying and uplifting times of my entire Christian life! I say, somewhat tongue in cheek, that I would go through the whole ordeal again to have that kind of sabbatical once more. It was a time of rich blessing while I recovered.

Today as I write this I feel like a kindergarten student coming back to my classmates having found a new color in his box of sixty-four crayons—a crayon that is brilliant, surprising, and radiant! I want everyone to see it. That crayon is the truth that *God is more than enough!*

Without this kind of contentment we easily progress on our way to disintegration on "The Way Down" chart. Let's look at this matter of contentment further.

THE EXCELLENCY OF CONTENTMENT

I want us to consider first of all *Paul's teaching* about contentment in 1 Timothy 6:6. He warns us that false teachers will promote an erroneous teaching that measures godliness by temporal prosperity—health and wealth. Paul says to stay away from that kind of teaching and understand rather that "godliness with contentment is great gain."

Paul teaches that true wealth in God's scheme of life is a godliness that is mature enough to produce contentment. Puritan Thomas Watson writes, "The doctrine of contentment is very superlative; and till we have learned this, we have not learned to be Christians." It is one of the chief marks of a believer who is living life truly as a Christian ought to live. Contentment testifies that the believer sees God as truly adequate for his daily challenges.

When I was a boy in the 1950s, it was common for families who had a dining room to put a bowl of plastic fruit in the center of the table. Plastic was still in its early developmental stages, and the waxy, cloudy look of the fruit meant you could tell it was plastic from across the room. Today you cannot tell the fruit in the bowl is plastic until you bite it or try to peel it.

Real fruit in a bowl also has an aroma that is distinctively pleasing. I believe that as humility is the *root* of all the graces in the Christian life, so contentment is the aroma of the collective *fruit* of the graces. It is the aroma of Christian maturity.

Paul's testimony had this kind of aroma. When Paul wrote the book of Philippians, he was in prison in Rome. Epaphroditus, perhaps the pastor of the assembly in Philippi, had gathered a "care package" for Paul from his people and set out for Rome to deliver it personally. While in Rome he got seriously ill—so ill that both Paul and Epaphroditus thought Epaphroditus would die. While they waited for him to recover in order to return home, Paul wrote the book we now call Philippians. Eventually Epaphroditus recovered and took the epistle home.

Imagine with me what it would have been like to be present in the Philippian congregation the first time Epaphroditus read the letter to them. Try to put yourself in that congregation as you listen to Paul's letter:

> I rejoiced in the Lord greatly that now at length you have revived your concern for me. You were indeed concerned for me, but you had no opportunity. Not that I am speaking of being in need, for I have learned in whatever situation I am to be content. I know how to be brought low, and I know how to abound. In any and every circumstance, I have learned the secret of facing plenty and hunger, abundance and need. I can do all things through him who strengthens me.
>
> Yet it was kind of you to share my trouble. And you Philippians yourselves know that in the beginning of the gospel, when I left Macedonia, no church entered into partnership with me in giving and receiving, except you only. Even in Thessalonica you sent me help for my needs once and again. Not that I seek the gift, but I seek the fruit that increases to your credit. I have received full payment, and more. I am well supplied, having received from Epaphroditus the gifts you sent, a fragrant offering, a sacrifice acceptable and pleasing to God. And my God will supply every need of yours according to his riches in glory in Christ Jesus. To our God and Father be glory forever and ever. Amen. (Philippians 4:10–20 ESV)

I can imagine after Epaphroditus ended his reading of this letter from their beloved apostle that a holy hush fell over the assembly as they let the words sink in. I can then imagine an elderly man at the back of the assembly slowly rise and request permission to speak to the group. Epaphroditus responded, "Of course, Justin, you know you can address this group anytime you wish." The elderly man shuffled to the front and began to speak.

"I know that many of you in this assembly have many times heard the account I am about to tell, but there are some new brothers and sisters in our group who have not heard this, and it is for their sakes that I tell it again.

"I want you to know that our beloved Paul—whose words you just heard—is writing these words out of his own experience. He doesn't just tell us to live this way. He lives this contentment at all times himself. I know—I was his jailer when he first came to this town.[2]

"He and his companion, Silas, had been arrested on false charges of disturbing the peace. They were flogged and then turned over to me for safekeeping. I remember how when I was putting them into the stocks—and I wasn't doing it too kindly, I'll tell you—Paul was telling me about Jesus, the Son of God, Who had died to pay for my sins. He wasn't concerned about his comfort; he was concerned about my soul. It was spooky to me. I got out of there as quickly as I could.

"And then there was that singing! I've heard lots of singing in my days as a jailer, but it was always the drunken singing of debauched lives. I had never heard anything like this. These men were singing to God and praising Him for His kindness to them. I didn't know what to think. I tried to occupy myself on the other side of the prison just to get away from them.

"But then there was that earthquake. It shook the whole place! The doors and the chains of the prisoners came off their anchors in the walls. I expected them all to escape, and I knew what that meant for me. Jailers who let prisoners of Rome escape were executed.

"I figured it was over for me, so I prepared to fall on my sword to take my life. Paul saw me and cried out for me to stop. He assured me that everyone was present and that none would escape.

"Instead of falling on my sword I ran to him and fell on my knees and asked him what I needed to do to have the salvation he had spoken of earlier. Here was a tortured and beaten prisoner comforting a hardened jailer and leading me to the feet of Jesus, where I accepted Him as my Savior, and I became a son of God.

"My point is this, dear people: I came to Christ because I saw the contentment of men who knew that their God was more than enough for them. Had they complained and cursed like the rest of the prisoners, I would have entered eternity that night without a Savior. Paul, indeed, knows how to be content in every situation, and I praise God for his contentment! My eternity hinged upon it."

I know the above conversation is entirely fictional, but Paul's effect on those around him because of his contentment is not. When I ponder these things, I wonder how many more unbelievers would come to Christ if the believers around them were content. This is the excellence of contentment. It is a crowning virtue—the aroma—of a mature walk with Christ and draws others to the Savior because it shows God to be more than enough for us.

THE ESSENCE OF CONTENTMENT

The definition of Christian contentment

The Greek word translated "content" in Philippians 4:11 is related to a similar word translated "contentment" in 1 Timothy 6:6. The Stoic and Cynic philosophers of New Testament times used the word to mean "self-satisfied," that is, they believed they didn't need anything outside of themselves because they were sufficient for themselves in one fashion or another. This is not the apostolic meaning of this word.

Paul was content, not because he had everything in himself but because His God had supplied everything he needed—in good times and in bad. Jeremiah Burroughs says, "Christian contentment is that sweet, inward, quiet, gracious frame of spirit, which freely submits to and delights in God's wise and fatherly disposal in every condition." It is not satisfied because it has found its fulfillment in something within the creature but in the Creator and His care for His creatures.

Did you catch those phrases: *submits to* and *delights in*? How often is that our response to the challenges of life that God Himself sends our way? Simply put, as I have already alluded, contentment means "I am satisfied with things as they are because God is more than enough for me."

The distinction of Christian contentment

This contentment is not a *passive resignation*. We cannot talk ourselves into this frame of mind by human logic alone—although we must remind ourselves of truths about God that apply to our situation. We *submit* ourselves to it by affirming divine truth. Christian contentment is not "I've done all I can. I guess I'll have to be content." An unbeliever can have that mindset, and its flaw is that God is not in the picture.

Neither is Christian contentment the same as a *passive personality*. Some people are never bothered by anything—except, of course, the interruption of their own comfort. The fact that a man seems to "roll with the punches" may not be an indication of virtue at all. It may be merely the outworking of his personality. Again, a contented Christian responds as he does because he sees God for Who He is.

Finally, Christian contentment is not an occasional response. It manifests itself in the mature Christian heart as a way of life. Watson again says, "Contentment doth not appear only now and then, as some stars which are seen but seldom; it is a settled temper of heart." Thus, "he is not a contented man who is so upon an occasion, and perhaps when he is pleased; but who is so constantly, when it is the habit and complexion of his soul."[5]

The doctrinal foundation of Christian contentment

The doctrine of Christian contentment rests upon the sufficiency of God. *It is inconceivable to a thoughtful and surrendered Christian that he should ever lack anything for his present happiness.* Pause to reflect on that statement for a few moments. This Christian understands that God Himself is more than enough for him. When David sang, "The Lord is my shepherd; I shall not want" (Psalm 23:1), he was testifying to this truth.

Henry W. Baker, who lived in the nineteenth century, captured well this thought in his wonderful hymn "The King of Love My Shepherd Is," based upon the sentiment of David's twenty-third psalm.

> The King of love my shepherd is,
> Whose goodness faileth never;
> I nothing lack if I am His
> And He is mine forever.
>
> Where streams of living water flow
> My ransomed soul He leadeth,
> And, where the verdant pastures grow,
> With food celestial feedeth.
>
> In death's dark vale I fear no ill
> With Thee, dear Lord, beside me;
> Thy rod and staff my comfort still,
> Thy cross before to guide me.
>
> And so through all the length of days
> Thy goodness faileth never:
> Good Shepherd, may I sing Thy praise
> Within Thy house forever.[6]

Baker understood full well that "through all the length of days" there is no need to fear because we who know Christ have a Good Shepherd.

Paul assured the Philippians that "my God shall supply all your need according to his riches in glory by Christ Jesus" (Philippians 4:19). That truth means that if we truly need something we will have it. It also means that *what we have is what we need*—whether deemed good or ill by us. God will provide whatever temporal provision we need or will in withholding it give us Himself and His grace to sustain us without it. In either case, we have what we need and can be content.

This is the divine logic of the truth that God cares for us and will supply all that we need in all situations. This is reality, and our lives must embrace what is true about God and His promises in order to live in reality.

Discontent means we have abandoned a biblical *view* of God and His absolute sufficiency. Discontent also means we have abandoned a biblical *response* to God of wholehearted surrender to His divine choices, which affect us. Do you see why it is so important to track your thinking and not your feeling?

As we saw in "The Way Down" chart, discontent is rooted in unbelief: "God has not done enough for me; God Himself is not enough for me. I need something more." This is the lie of unbelief and begins the process of our own disintegration and of our withholding from God the glory due to Him from our lives.

THE ENEMY OF CONTENTMENT

The Bible presents covetousness as the polar opposite of contentment in Hebrews 13:5.

> Let your [lifestyle] be without covetousness [in this case, the love of money]; and be content with such things as ye have: for he hath said, I will never leave thee, nor forsake thee.

Covetousness says, "*Who* God is does not satisfy me; *what* He has supplied does not satisfy me. I must have something *more*." If God's statement "I will never leave thee, nor forsake thee" in the verse above doesn't quiet your soul when you hear it, you don't know well the One

Who is speaking. You must pursue knowing God—the topic of the next part of this book.

This discontent is how Lucifer fell and along with him the angels who followed him in the primal rebellion against God. They thought they needed something more. This is how our first parents, Adam and Eve, fell. They thought they needed something more. This is how Israel in the wilderness fell. They thought they needed something more. This is why churches split and marriages fail. This is why children and employees rebel. They think they need something more.

This lust for more is not a small issue. Where there is the smoke of whining, complaining, griping, and bitterness, there is the fire of covetousness—the demand for something more. The fire has the aroma of sulfur about it because its source is hell itself.

The root of this covetousness, as we have seen, is unbelief. It cries, "God is not enough! I must have more!" In contrast, believing what God has said about Himself is the foundation of contentment. Take some time to meditate upon Paul's statement in Romans 15:13. He says,

> Now the God of hope fill you with all joy and peace in believing, that ye may abound in hope through the power of the Holy [Spirit].

Paul says you can live a hope-filled life filled with joy and peace if you believe what is true about God. Incidentally, if you take joy and peace and put them into a blender and turn the knob to high, you will come out with a smoothie that tastes like contentment. Contentment—the blend of joy and peace—comes only through believing the right thing about God.

If God is the biggest thing in your life, you don't need anything more, nor do you want it. He is more than enough. And conversely, if God is not enough to satisfy you, then nothing will be enough for you.

Real Christian liberty is walking through a mall and not seeing anything you think you have to have. This is true freedom from lust—and only a Christian with a God-besotted soul can know it. Christian liberty is rejoicing with your friend who has something you don't have, be it possessions, good health, position, or relationship—and you don't envy him. This is Christian maturity; this is contentment.

WHAT DO YOU WANT
WRITTEN ON YOUR TOMBSTONE?

I want to close this discussion of contentment by relating to you an incident of the time when God taught me how important it is to know Him. I was in college, and I had heard someone say, "You are not ready to live until you know what you want written on your tombstone." The point was that you don't know how to live your life now if you don't know how you want it to end up. The divine logic of that statement bored deep into my soul.

I went back to my room, took out a blank sheet of paper, drew a crude tombstone on it, and pondered that challenge over the next several days. I asked God to show me what was important enough to Him that it should characterize my life. I searched the Scriptures during that time, and God finally directed me to Jeremiah 9:23–24, which says,

> Thus saith the Lord, Let not the wise man glory in his wisdom, neither let the mighty man glory in his might, let not the rich man glory in his riches: but let him that glorieth glory in this, that he understandeth and knoweth me.

Immediately, I knew that was the truth I was looking for. I wrote on the paper tombstone, "Here lies a man who knew God." I'm not in any way demanding that my family put this on my tombstone, but I determined then that I want to live in such a way that those watching would conclude that knowing God is important to me.

After the study on contentment following heart surgery I decided that I needed to amend my tombstone marker to read, "Here lies a man who knew God and found Him to be more than enough." Paul had that testimony and so can we; we have the same God.

Noisy souls are discontent. They must repent of their covetousness and meditate upon the truths we will discuss in the following chapters to have a quiet soul. You must know God well enough to be satisfied that He Himself is enough for you.

Take Time to Reflect

1. The statement was made in this chapter that "It is inconceivable to a thoughtful and surrendered Christian that he should ever lack anything for his present happiness." What do we know about God that makes this statement true?

2. Why does the quote above include the words *thoughtful* and *surrendered*? In other words, why are those words necessary for the statement to be true?

3. Can you say that your lifestyle is without covetousness (Hebrews 13:5)? If not, in what areas of your life are you most tempted to be discontent and covetous?

Chapter Seven

BEHOLDING THE GOD OF LOVE

What shall we say then to these things? If God be for us, who can be against us? He that spared not his own Son, but delivered him up for us all, how shall he not with him also freely give us all things? . . . [No,] in all these things we are more than conquerors through him that loved us. (Romans 8:31–32, 37)

Most of us who are parents and grandparents carry pictures of our children and grandchildren in our wallets, our PDAs or cell phones. We like to be ready when others inquire about our loved ones—and sometimes, even when they haven't inquired. In a similar fashion—but for different reasons—we all carry around in the "wallet" of our mind a picture of God. That picture is the most important thing about us. A. W. Tozer addresses this in his wonderful book *The Knowledge of the Holy.*

> What comes into our minds when we think about God is the most important thing about us. . . . Were we able to extract from any man a complete answer to the question, "What comes into your mind when you think about God?" we might predict with certainty the spiritual future of that man. . . . The man who comes to a right belief about God is relieved of ten thousand temporal problems, for he sees at once that these have to do with matters which at the most cannot concern him for very long.

> Among the sins to which the human heart is prone, hardly any other is more hateful to God than idolatry, for idolatry is at bottom a libel on His character. The idolatrous heart assumes that God is other than He is—in itself a monstrous sin—and

substitutes for the true God one made after its own likeness.
. . . Let us beware lest we in our pride accept the erroneous
notion that idolatry consists only in kneeling before visible
objects of adoration, and that civilized peoples are therefore
free from it. The essence of idolatry is the entertainment of
thoughts about God that are unworthy of Him.[1]

Were we able to project your picture of God onto a screen in front of
your church, we would be able to predict how prone you are to worry
and how susceptible you are to bitterness and unforgiveness. We could
also tell how easily you become discouraged and how much time you
probably spend in self-pitying thoughts that lead to despair. Your pro-
pensity to lustful thoughts and greed would be readily evident. All of
these are direct indicators of your view of God.

In this chapter and in several to follow we will look briefly at some
crucial aspects of God's nature in an effort to help you develop a more
proper view of God. A few short chapters will not do justice to our
amazing God, but they will point you in the right direction. The believer comes to know God well as he spends much time directly in
God's Word, where God has revealed Himself to the seeking soul.

I want to start with one aspect of God's nature that I think is of ut-
most importance—the love of God. Most of us don't have much trouble
believing that God is powerful—especially as we look around at His
amazing creation, but we often question his love for us. Believers who
do not know well the love of God ask questions like the following:

"If God loves me, why do I hurt so much?" or "Why isn't my
marriage working?" or "Why can't I get lasting victory over my
sin?"

"If God loves me, why did he let Mom die?" or "Why do I have
cancer?" or "Why don't I have a spouse?"

"If God loves me, why would he let me be abused as a child?"
or "Why can't I pay my bills?"

It is interesting that no attribute of God is more evident in the Scriptures than His love, yet no attribute of God is doubted as quickly when
life is challenging than His love. To help us see this amazing quality of

God, let's start with one of Paul's statements about the love of God in Romans 8.

> What then shall we say to these things? If God is for us, who can be against us? He who did not spare his own Son but gave him up for us all, how will he not also with him graciously give us all things? Who shall bring any charge against God's elect? It is God who justifies. Who is to condemn? Christ Jesus is the one who died—more than that, who was raised—who is at the right hand of God, who indeed is interceding for us. Who shall separate us from the love of Christ? Shall tribulation, or distress, or persecution, or famine, or nakedness, or danger, or sword? As it is written,
>
> "For your sake we are being killed all the day long; we are regarded as sheep to be slaughtered."
>
> No, in all these things we are more than conquerors through him who loved us. For I am sure that neither death nor life, nor angels nor rulers, nor things present nor things to come, nor powers, nor height nor depth, nor anything else in all creation, will be able to separate us from the love of God in Christ Jesus our Lord. (ESV)

Can you see how this truth should be such a stabilizing factor in the human soul? No man can have a genuinely God-taught contentment about his life who has not seen from God Himself through His Word the love of God for him. Ephesians 3 teaches that a Spirit-taught understanding of the length and breadth and depth of this love is the source of spiritual strengthening in the inner man (verses 14–21). We must come to know this amazing love!

When our three daughters were preschool age, they were frightened of Tinker Bell, my parents' very large Siamese cat. As soon as they heard the crunch of our car tires on the gravel driveway of my parent's home across town, they would ask, "Is Tinker Bell in the house?" They did not want to go into the house if Tinker Bell was inside.

This fear was a bit puzzling for me at first since I had grown up around animals on the farm. But when I looked at the situation through their eyes, I understood. Tinker Bell was in proportion to them as a bobcat would be to me. I certainly wouldn't want to meet an unpredictable bobcat in the wild, and they didn't want to be near Tinker Bell for the same reason.

The only way they would approach Tinker Bell was if I would hold him on my lap and invite them to "Come, pet the kitty." They would gingerly reach out a little hand and cautiously make one or two strokes and then run away triumphantly declaring, "Mommy, Mommy, I pet the kitty! I pet the kitty!"

Now the question is "What made them feel safe?" It was not just my size—the fact that I was bigger and more powerful than Tinker Bell—because my father, their grandfather, could put Tinker Bell in his lap and invite them to pet the cat and they wouldn't do it. They could easily see that grandpa was bigger than the kitty, but at three and five they still had not been around their grandpa enough to know his love and care for them. They not only knew that I was bigger than the kitty but also knew that I loved them enough to protect them from danger.

In a similar fashion, *the man who knows that God is powerful but does not yet really know God's love will still be filled with fears.* In fact, having a God Who is supremely powerful is no comfort at all if you don't think He likes you.

THE ESSENCE OF GOD'S LOVE (WHAT IS IT?)

God's love is a subset of His greater attribute of goodness. The fact that God is good has two aspects.

That God is good, first of all, means that God is excellent. He answers in all His parts and attributes to the ideal of what God should be like. Good used in this way is what we mean when we say we have a "good" car, computer, child, marriage, roommate, or job.

This aspect of God—His excellence—is more important than you might imagine at first glance. If God were not excellent in wisdom, we could rightly question His decisions. If He were not excellent in righteousness, we might doubt the validity and necessity of His commands. If we don't have an accurate view of what a "good" God is like, we will have the wrong expectations for him. Let me illustrate it this way.

Years ago a freshman came to BJU from an extremely wealthy family. Shannon (not her real name) grew up with a governess who did everything for her. The governess curled her hair, laid out her clothes, drew her bath water, made her bed, brought her snacks, listened to her lessons, and so forth.

When Shannon came to the residence halls, she expected that her roommates would continue to do those things for her. In fact, when they were not immediately inclined to do those things for her, she thought they were not "good" roommates.

Fortunately, she had a spiritually minded upperclassman in her room who saw Shannon's need and in order to build relational bridges to her did many of those things for her in the beginning. She, as you might expect, had a powerful impact upon Shannon.

The point I want you to see is that Shannon's expectations of her roommates were skewed by her misunderstanding about what made for a "good" roommate. Many Christians also are quite disappointed when God does not come through for them in a way that they think a "good" God should operate. They don't have an accurate view of God.

The reality is that God gets an A++ in being God! He is excellent—answering in all parts to the ideal. When we think of Him as deficient in some way—and give Him a poor grade—we are guilty of the idolatry that Tozer spoke of at the beginning of this chapter. We must not allow our minds to entertain unholy thoughts of God. We not only dishonor Him—the greatest offense—but subject ourselves to living in a world with a picture of God that does not correspond to reality and bring about our own disintegration.

That God is good also means that God is benevolent, that is, "He is good to me!" Satan was able to tempt Adam and Eve to disobey God by casting doubt upon God's benevolence. Satan wanted them to think that because God had withheld something from them He was not being good. We, too, place ourselves in an extremely vulnerable position spiritually if we at all doubt the goodness—the love—of God. We must beg God to show us His love through His Word and through His actions towards us.

The first time I was struck with the love of God in this way I was a freshman at Bob Jones University. I had come to college in 1970 in rebellion and at the insistence of my parents to attend a Christian college for at least a year. I had agreed to stay the one year and then intended to return home to pursue my own dreams and former sins—dreams and sins I knew were not God's calling on my life.

In high school I had dishonored God and my parents in many ways. I played my guitar in a rock group against my parent's wishes—and God's. Many weekend evenings I didn't come home. I told my parents I was working and staying overnight at my boss's apartment. Sometimes I was, but often I wasn't. I began to steal whenever I saw something I wanted. I stole from my boss, my friends, from businesses in town, and from my high school. I had met a girl I thought I wanted to marry, and once my freshman year was over, I was going back home to pick up where I had left off in my rebellious lifestyle.

I rejoice that God had other plans for me! I came under great conviction under the chapel preaching at college. During the second semester of my freshman year, BJU released a full-length feature film *Flame in the Wind*. I went to the opening of the film and came under such great conviction from God I could hold out no longer. I responded to the invitation and made everything right with God.

I had much I had to make right with my parents, my high school, my friends, my boss, and Bob Jones University. I began repaying people for the things I had stolen and reconciling with authorities I had disobeyed. I did all I could to make things right with the people I had wronged.

It was in the midst of all of this that I was walking back to my residence hall one evening. The campus was quiet and as I walked over the bridge spanning the fountain on front campus I paused under the starlit sky and reflected on where I was. It occurred to me that there was only one reason I was standing on the campus of Bob Jones University instead of being in jail for theft or married to the wrong woman or instead of a thousand other disasters that could have come my way in my rebellion. I was standing there because there was a God in heaven Who loved me! I will never forget that moment.

He had rescued me! He didn't have to, but He did! I could cry with the psalmist, "The Lord is good to all: and his tender mercies are over all his works" (Psalm 145:9). "The earth is full of the goodness of the Lord" (Psalm 33:5). I could identify with David, when he exclaimed, "O give thanks unto the Lord, for he is good: for his mercy endureth for ever" (Psalm 107:1). The rest of that psalm recounts several instances of God's deliverance for Israel. Each instances ends with the refrain, "Oh that men would praise the Lord for his goodness, and for his wonderful works to the children of men" (Psalm 107:8, 15, 21, 31).

David closed that psalm with the words "Whoso is wise, and will observe these things, even they shall understand the lovingkindness of the Lord" (verse 43).

I have often come into my office in the administration building of BJU and when I see the sign on my door that says "Dean of Students," I exclaim to God, "You know I'm not good enough to be doing this." He immediately reminds me, "You're not here because you have been good; you are here because I am good." What a wonderful God He is!

I to this day cannot hold back the tears when I reflect on Psalm 103, where David said, "He hath not dealt with us after our sins; nor rewarded us according to our iniquities. For as the heaven is high above the earth, so great is his mercy toward them that fear him. As far as the east is from the west, so far hath he removed our transgressions from us" (verses 10–12).

These are wonderful words about the lovingkindness of our God to us poor sinners, who deserve nothing more than His wrath! When you begin to truly know God, you will discover that your sinfulness is far worse than you thought but that His grace and love are far more amazing than you ever imagined!

If you are quick to defend yourself or blame others, you don't know your own heart well. And conversely, if the knowledge of your sin sends you into the depths of self-pity and hopelessness, you have not yet seen the marvelous grace of God to repentant sinners. The knowledge of our sinfulness should humble us, but the knowledge of the cross-work of the Lord Jesus should produce an even greater humility that such a One should die for us and an even greater love for the One Who did such a wondrous thing for us.

God's love is His personal communication to a rational creature of His benevolence by giving Himself for the highest good of that creature. Love is sometimes described as a self-sacrificing choice to meet the genuine spiritual needs of another. We must meditate upon these truths and "argue ourselves back to reality." We start on the "The Way Down" when we listen to our sinful hearts when we should be arguing against our sinful thoughts.

THE EXTENT OF GOD'S LOVE (HOW VAST IS IT?)

Paul prayed in Ephesians 3:18 that believers would be able to comprehend the dimensions of God's love—its breadth, length, and depth. Let me give you two thoughts to consider about the extent of God's love.

First, you cannot do anything that will cause God to love you more than He already does. Since God loves us with perfect love, He cannot improve on it. There are many believers who try to do all sorts of good things— live holy lives before God, render extraordinary service to God, and so forth—all in the attempt to get God to love and accept them more than He does. The truth is that God loves us in the same manner in which He loves His Son, Jesus Christ. We are told in John 17:23 that Jesus said to His Father, "[Thou] hast loved them, as thou hast loved me." That's an astonishing statement!

The reason it is true is that God can love anyone only one way—with perfect love. We get His blessing and attention not because we have become worthy of His love but because He is a certain kind of person.

When our daughters were in preschool, we would pick them up for lunch and they would often greet us waving a paper upon which they had drawn something—a picture of Mommy and Daddy or of the whole family. It was typical four-year-old artwork.

We would try to be as encouraging as possible—while being honest, of course. We would say, "Honey, that's wonderful! I can tell you really worked hard on that." Or "Honey, that's great! It has so many beautiful colors in it." I remember one time one daughter followed up with a penetrating question, "Daddy, can you take it to work and hang it in your office?" I replied, "Sweetie, the people who love you most live in our house. Let's take it home and hang it on the refrigerator so that the people who love you most can see it all the time." With that she was satisfied. Her artwork will not hang in the Louvre because it lacks artistic quality, but it will hang in our home because of our love for her.

What I want you to take away from this scenario is this truth. My daughters did not get glowing commendations from their parents because the artwork was so stunning and compelling. They got it because their parents loved them and wanted to encourage them for doing their best.

When I get to heaven and stand before the Lord Jesus, I want very much to hear Him say to me, "Well done, thou good and faithful servant" (Matthew 25:21). I know, however, if I ever hear those words it will not be because my "artwork"—my personal holiness—is so stunning that God is compelled to praise my life. If I hear those words, it will be because a loving Father is encouraging a son who tried his best for His Father. It will be because the Father is that loving, not because my holiness is that compelling. God will praise what He Himself produced in and through me as expressions of His love.

Secondly, you cannot do anything that will cause Him to love you less. We can certainly grieve the heart of God by our sin, but that does not diminish His love for us. Furthermore, our sin does not surprise God and make Him reconsider His judgment in making us His child.

Most Christians don't gamble—except when they buy a car. When you buy a car, you might think you know what you are getting, but you really don't. Even new cars are subject to recalls and factory defects. But when God "bought" us with the blood of His own Son, He knew exactly what He was getting right up front.

His love is everlasting. Listen to what He says through Jeremiah, the prophet. "Yea, I have loved thee with an everlasting love: therefore with lovingkindness have I drawn thee" (31:3).

Everlasting love is unchangeable; it is everlasting. This is great news! Seeing the everlasting dimension of God's love is one of the most stabilizing truths you can know. Though we can understand something of God's love in thinking about its unchangeableness, nothing reveals His love like Calvary.

THE EVIDENCE OF GOD'S LOVE
(HOW DO I KNOW HE LOVES ME?)

The most notable expression of God's love is the work of His Son, Jesus, on our behalf on the cross of Calvary. It is the fullest demonstration of His love.

> But God shows his love for us in that while we were still sinners, Christ died for us. (Romans 5:8 ESV)

> In this the love of God was made manifest among us, that God sent his only Son into the world, so that we might live through

him. In this is love, not that we have loved God but that he loved us and sent his Son to be the propitiation for our sins. (1 John 4:9–10 ESV)

A few years back I was struck with Paul's statement about the cross in Galatians 6:14: "But God forbid that I should [boast] save in the cross of our Lord Jesus Christ." I pondered that verse much and reflected on the thought that this cross was far more central to Paul's life than it was to mine. I determined that there was still much, then, about this cross that I did not understand and decided to spend a weekend meditating upon Isaiah 53 asking God to show me the glory of this cross.

I cleared away a Saturday and spent the morning meditating on the chapter and studying a few commentaries on the passage. All the while I was praying that God would allow me to "comprehend . . . what is the breadth, and length, and depth, and height; and to know the love of Christ, which passeth knowledge" (Ephesians 3:18–19).

Midway through the afternoon God's Spirit opened my eyes in a fuller fashion than I had known before of God's great love for me! I had always respected and valued what God did for me on the cross, but I had never seen it with the kind of illuminated understanding God gave me that afternoon. I saw in a new and far more powerful and personal way that "He was wounded for *my* transgressions! He was bruised for *my* iniquities! The chastisement of *my* sin was upon Him, and with His stripes *I* was healed" (Isaiah 53:5)! The realization was overwhelming, and all I could do was sob out my gratitude to God for such great love for such a great sinner. Reflecting on the truth of His love at Calvary brings tears to my eyes to this day. I'll never forget the lesson—nor do I ever want to forget it.

Many of us have been wounded by the sins of others against us. All of us have been wounded by our own sins. We can spend a lifetime of grief and regret if we are not careful. We must stop looking at our own wounds and start looking at His! Jesus is the One Who bears our griefs and carries our sorrows. (Isaiah 53:4

No wonder so many of the hymns of the past focused so often on Jesus as Redeemer and Savior. It is "Amazing Love" "that thou my God shouldst die for me." We should each "stand amazed in the presence of Jesus the Nazarene, and wonder how He could love me, a sinner—condemned, unclean." We each should exclaim, "How marvelous, how wonderful is my Savior's love for me!"

This is the One Who says to us in Hebrews 4:15–16,

> For we have not an high priest which cannot be touched with the feelings of our infirmities; but was in all points tempted like as we are, yet without sin. Let us therefore come boldly unto the throne of grace that we may obtain mercy, and find grace to help in time of need.

There are many things about God and His ways that we do not understand; but since Jesus died for sinners at that cross, it must ever remain a blasphemy to think, "God does not love!"

THE EFFECT OF GOD'S LOVE
(WHAT DIFFERENCE DOES IT MAKE?)

The impact of the love of God upon a fallen but redeemed creature is varied.

Matthew 6:24–34 and 1 John 4:16–18 teach us that God's love *banishes our fears.*

The apostle John also tells us that God's love for us *compels us to love others* (1 John 4:7–11).

Paul proclaims that the love of God *compels us to great energy and evangelism* (2 Corinthians 5:14–15).

And we see in John's final book, the Revelation, that the love of the Lamb of God for sinners *inspires true worship* (5:9–14).

The truth is that God does not just love sinners—God loves me! That is a gripping, compelling, truth. It is reality. If you are "afraid of the cat"—the dangerous possibilities of life—you don't yet understand well the love of the One holding the cat.

Begin right away memorizing and praying Ephesians 3:14–19. God wants you to know His love, but the fact that Paul prays for the Ephesians to know God's love is an indication that to know God's love in the way Paul wants us to know it is not automatic. We must ask God to open our eyes in a fresh way to the love of our marvelous God. I invite you to "taste and see that the Lord is good" because "blessed is the man that trusteth in him" (Psalm 34:8).

Your soul will rest when you know that *God's love is more than enough for you.*

Take Time to Reflect

1. In the "wallet" of your mind where you keep your picture of God, does that picture include a generous awareness of God's love for you personally or is the fact that God loves you something that is difficult for you to grasp? Explain your answer.

2. Read carefully Psalm 107, noticing the cycle of Israel's rebellion, chastening, cries for help, and finally God's deliverance. After you finish reflectively reading the passage, write down the similarities of that cycle to the course of your own life.

Chapter Eight

BEHOLDING THE GOD OF MERCY

But God, who is rich in mercy, for his great love wherewith he loved us, even when we were dead in sins, hath [made us alive] together with Christ. (Ephesians 2:4–5)

The American public was rightly disturbed when former president Bill Clinton pardoned several unsavory friends in his last days in office. He offered clemency to billionaire Marc Rich, who was living in exile in Switzerland. Rich was charged with evading more than $48 million in taxes, with participating in illegal oil deals, and with other counts of fraud. Clinton wanted to extend him some mercy.

The response of most of us was "This isn't mercy; this is a travesty of justice!" Unfortunately, many today misunderstand the true nature of mercy. Often school officials, state prosecutors, and parents are charged with being unmerciful if they do not let a guilty person off the hook. They hear cries like, "Why can't you give him a second chance? He said he's sorry!" Or "If you have forgiven someone, why do you let him suffer?"

As a result adulterous pastors are allowed to return to their pulpits. Sentimental school board members tie the hands of school administrators in disciplinary matters, and parents hesitate to impose consequences of misbehavior on their children.

In contrast to these modern situations, think with me about how God administered mercy. Was God unmerciful when he let King David suffer for the rest of his life under the consequences of murdering Uriah, his general, and committing adultery with Uriah's wife—even when David sought and was granted forgiveness? Was God unmerciful to Moses when He did not let Israel's leader enter the Promised Land after striking the rock instead of speaking to it? Was God unmerciful to Adam and Eve for expelling them from the garden and cursing their labors even though they obviously faced their sin and accepted His skins of covering for their nakedness?

Is God unmerciful because He arranges these extended consequences for His people even after He forgives their sin? These kinds of questions trouble us unless we understand God's view of mercy.

Paul calls God, "The Father of mercies" in 2 Corinthians 1:3, and David extols God's mercies in many of his psalms. Any misunderstanding of mercy will skew our view of God, but the right view of God will correct a deficient view of mercy. Let's see what the Scriptures have to say to us about God's unfailing mercies.

THE DEFINITION OF MERCY

Mercy has many facets but basically mercy is *rescuing someone from his miserable condition*. Jesus' account of the Good Samaritan in Luke 10 clears up much of the misunderstanding. A lawyer had asked Jesus how he could inherit eternal life. Jesus replied that he needed to love God with all his heart and his neighbor as himself. In order to deflect responsibility the lawyer responded, "Who is my neighbor?" Jesus told him the following story (Luke 10:30–35).

> A certain man went down from Jerusalem to Jericho, and fell among thieves, which stripped him of his raiment, and wounded him, and departed, leaving him half dead. And by chance there came down a certain priest that way: and when he saw him, he passed by on the other side. And likewise a Levite, when he was at the place, came and looked on him, and passed by on the other side. But a certain Samaritan, as he journeyed, came where he was: and when he saw him, he had compassion on him, and went to him, and bound up his wounds, pouring in oil and wine, and set him on his own beast, and brought him to an inn, and took care of him. And on the morrow when he departed, he took out two pence, and gave them to the host, and said unto him, Take care of him; and whatsoever thou spendest more, when I come again, I will repay thee.

When Jesus finished the story, He challenged the lawyer to tell him which of the three men—the priest, the Levite, or the Samaritan—

was a neighbor to the unfortunate man. The lawyer replied, "He that shewed mercy on Him" (10:37).

This is a curious response if mercy is defined as "not giving someone what he deserves." Some think mercy means giving an offender a second chance. That doesn't fit here either. It is clear from this passage that mercy at its core means rescuing someone from his miserable condition. It can mean more than this, but it cannot mean less. In order for us to have quiet souls we must know that *God delights in mercy*; He delights in rescuing us from our miserable conditions! What hope this should breathe into our troubled souls!

We must further understand that not all miserable conditions are created equal; God has priorities about miserable conditions.

For example, suppose two men arrive at the emergency room of a small hospital at the same time. Both are in extreme pain. One is having a heart attack, and the other has a broken arm from a sports accident. If the doctor can help only one at a time, which one will he attend to first? Of course, he will help the heart patient first. Though both men are in great pain, one's condition is life-threatening and gets a higher priority for treatment. We would think the doctor incompetent if he chose to set the broken arm while the heart attack victim died.

The Scriptures show us the ultimate misery as the condition of the lost in hell—and the condition of those who are bound for hell. Nothing can be more miserable than eternal torment.

The second most miserable condition is that of a believer out of fellowship with God. Psalm 32 and 38 make this clear. Both the Old and New Testaments reveal the extent God will go to restore His people when they fall. He loves them too much to allow them to remain in their miserable condition of estrangement from their God and Savior. Interestingly, these first two miserable conditions involve one's spiritual state.

Lastly, the least miserable condition of all is the physical and emotional suffering of this present life. Though I would never minimize the horrible suffering that many—including many of God's people—go through, it is a "broken bone" when compared to the "heart attack" of the previous two conditions.

The truth of this is seen in the fact that God will often induce physical suffering to rescue one of His children from the misery of his or her distance from Him. Witness Israel's captivity, the suffering already mentioned of King David when he covered his sin, and the Lord's own statement "As many as I love, I rebuke and chasten" (Revelation 3:19).

The Bible is clear that not all suffering is a result of sin, however. Paul's "thorn in the flesh" was given to him for his spiritual benefit (2 Corinthians 12:7–10) and was not a result of God's chastening. In either case, the point is that *eternal and spiritual issues always have priority over temporal and physical issues.*

OUR MISERABLE CONDITION

The biblical record is clear about the extent God has gone to save us from our most miserable condition—condemnation to the eternal penalty for our sin in hell. Think carefully as Paul reasons through the divine logic of Ephesians 2:1–3.

> And you hath he [made alive], who were dead in trespasses and sins; wherein in time past ye walked according to the course of this world, according to the prince of the power of the air, the spirit that now [energizes] the children of disobedience: among whom also we all had our [lifestyle] in times past in the lusts of our flesh, fulfilling the desires of the [body] and of the mind; and were by nature the children of wrath, even as others.

This account of our miserable condition reminds me of the classic book *Old Yeller*, where author Fred Gipson describes the miserable condition of a rabid dog. The story is about a Texas rancher in 1859 who left his family for several months to sell cattle in Kansas. He left his fifteen-year-old son, Travis, in charge.

The day after the father left, a stray yellow dog caused much trouble, and Travis tried to chase it away. The dog, however, adopted the family and protected them, even risking his own life. He saved Travis's younger brother, Arliss, from an angry bear and rescued Travis from attacks by wild pigs.

When Old Yeller fought a rabid wolf to protect the family, he was bitten by the wolf. Travis penned Old Yeller up to see if the disease developed.

Sure enough, Old Yeller had rabies, and Travis had to shoot his beloved dog.

Destroying the dog was the only merciful thing to do to relieve the dog's suffering and, more importantly, the only merciful thing to do for the rest of the farm animals and for the family. Notice the parallels to our condition as described in Ephesians 2.

Paul says we were under a death sentence. We were "dead in trespasses and sins" (verse 1). We had not been bitten by a rabid dog but by a serpent and awaited our destruction. Like a rabid dog we were controlled by a hostile force. We lived under the influence of the "course of this world, according to the prince of the power of the air" (verse 2). Jesus said of us, "Ye are of your father the devil, and the lusts of your father ye will do" (John 8:44).

Like a rabid dog whose central nervous system under viral attack produces irrational and violent behavior and severe throat and mouth spasms, every part of our nature was contaminated by sin's power. We could yield only to the "desires of the [body] and of the mind" (verse 3). Every part of fallen man is tainted by the fall—his emotions, his will, his mind, and his affections. Consequently, we were slated for destruction.

The wrath of God that we justly deserve is not some uncontrolled emotional outburst of God's temper but the calculated decision to eliminate sin and protect His redeemed creation. As in the case of Old Yeller's destruction, judgment is the only merciful and the only righteous thing to do for unrepentant sinners.

GOD'S MERCIFUL INTERVENTION

But our Creator takes pleasure in rescuing His human creatures. Listen to Paul's account of God's merciful efforts from Ephesians 2:4–10.

> But God, who is rich in mercy, for his great love wherewith he loved us, even when we were dead in sins, hath [made us alive] together with Christ, (by grace ye are saved;) and hath raised us up together, and made us sit together in heavenly places in Christ Jesus: that in the ages to come he might shew the exceeding riches of his grace in his kindness toward us through Christ Jesus. For by grace are ye saved through faith; and that not of yourselves: it is the gift of God: not of works, lest any man should boast. For

we are his workmanship, created in Christ Jesus unto good works, which God hath before ordained that we should walk in them.

We were condemned and waiting execution, but now we are made alive and await glorification. God is "rich in mercy" and is naturally disposed to rescue us. It is not something He must talk Himself into; He delights to do so! Here's how Jeremiah described it.

For I know the thoughts that I think toward you, saith the Lord, thoughts of peace [of welfare], and not of evil, to give you an expected end [a future and a hope]. (29:11)

God's plan to rescue us is multifaceted! *He changes the decision against us.* Though we were slated for eternal death, He gives us eternal life.

He changes the disposition within us. Though we were by nature His enemies, He made us new creations in Christ (2 Corinthians 5:17). We are no longer on a downward "rabid" path that leads to destruction. Old things have passed away and the new has come. We are heading in a different direction. God is transforming us into the likeness of His Son (Romans 8:29).

And finally, *He changes the destiny of our soul.* Though we justly deserved eternal damnation, He "made us sit together in heavenly places" (verse 6). We who know Christ as our Redeemer still live on earth, but our home address has changed!

This is an astonishing plan! For the growing, surrendered believer, there is nothing he delights to hear of more than this "Old, old story of Jesus and His love." It thrilled Paul too. When he reviewed the amazing mercy of God to sinners He cried out in Romans 11:33,

O the depth of the riches both of the wisdom and knowledge of God! how unsearchable are his judgments, and his ways past finding out!

Some implications

This teaching about God's mercy has some important implications.

First, God rescued us from our miserable condition *to show the greatness of His goodness.* Mercy, like love, is a subset of God's goodness. Why did He do this? Listen to the words of the apostle Paul.

> That in the ages to come he might shew the exceeding riches of
> his grace in his kindness toward us through Christ Jesus. (Ephe-
> sians 2:7)

One day in the future God will display before all the created beings
of heaven and earth the transformed "rabid" dogs He rescued—His
church—and all will see "the exceeding riches of his grace." Everyone
will see the stunning wisdom of His plan and the great power that
brought it to pass and "every knee [will] bow, of things in heaven, and
things in earth, and things under the earth; and . . . every tongue
[will] confess that Jesus Christ is Lord, to the glory of God the Father"
(Philippians 2:9–11). We will all stand before Him with "shiny coats
and wagging tails" and praise Him for our rescue! We should join the
psalmist, who cried,

> O give thanks unto the Lord, for he is good: for his mercy en-
> dureth for ever [He will always delight in rescuing]. . . . Oh that
> men would praise the Lord for his goodness, and for his wonderful
> works to the children of men. . . . Whoso is wise, and will observe
> these things [all these deliverances talked about earlier in the
> psalm], even they shall understand the lovingkindness [mercy] of
> the Lord. (Psalm 107)

He rescued us to show the greatness of His goodness. But there are
other reasons for the rescue.

God rescued us from our miserable condition *to make us useful again.*
You may feel like anything but useful right now. You might be wondering, "How could God ever use me? My life is so messed up. I can
scarcely put one decent thought in front of the other without being
tortured by a dozen wicked ones. I have so many bad habits to overcome
and so many fractured relationships to rebuild. I am a mess!"

Friend, this is the point of this whole discussion. God delights to show
mercy to us; He delights to rescue people from their miserable conditions—especially from their miserable spiritual conditions. You and I
cannot save ourselves from hell, and we cannot save ourselves from
our noisy souls either. We need—and have—a merciful Savior, Who
delights in rescuing us!

God places some responsibility upon us, however. He did not cancel
our destruction and give us the antidote so that we can live any way

we please now. Our rescue compels a certain kind of response from us. Here's how Paul put it in 2 Corinthians 5:14–15.

> For the love of Christ [controls] us; because we thus judge [we've come to this conclusion], that if one died for all, then were all dead: and that he died for all, that they which live should not henceforth live unto themselves, but unto him which died for them, and rose again.

God also rescued us *to fulfill the original purpose for our creation*—to glorify God by fearing, loving, and serving Him. That isn't possible in our rabid state. But it is possible now that we have His own Spirit changing us into His image (2 Corinthians 3:18; 4:16–18). Teaching us how to quiet our soul is part of the renewal He wants to perform in us so that we will be increasingly useful to Him in His gospel work here on the earth.

Lastly, He rescued us from our miserable condition *to involve us in rescuing others from their miserable condition through the same gospel that rescued us.* Are you bringing the gospel to the lost? Rabies is a terminal disease that ends with horrible torment of the victim. Eternal life without Christ is an eternal torment. Jesus died to save sinners. If you truly have been redeemed by His blood from your sin, your life must be about living before and proclaiming the gospel to the lost around you.

Are you confronting sinning believers with their sins? Paul said in Galatians 6:1,

> Brethren, if a man be overtaken in a fault, ye which are spiritual [those of you walking in the Spirit], restore such an one in the spirit of meekness; considering thyself, lest thou also be tempted.

Imagine what our churches and Christian families would be like if we took this responsibility to rescue each other seriously. We would be examining ourselves to remove the "beams" out of our own eyes so that we could see clearly to remove the "splinters" out of the eyes of others (Matthew 7:3–5). Both we and they would be better for it!

Are you comforting those who suffer physically or emotionally? So many around us need an encouraging word, a helping hand, and a praying friend. These are all part of the merciful rescue work God has given us to do on the earth.

My main point in this discussion of the mercy of God is for you to see the goodness of our wonderful God to us. Your soul will continue to be noisy unless you know Him as the God of mercy—the One Who delights in rescuing you from your miserable condition. This is His disposition toward you. Your soul can rest because *God's mercy is more than enough for you.*

Take Time to Reflect

1. The basic definition of mercy is "rescuing someone from his or her miserable condition." "Not all 'miserable conditions' are created equal; God has priorities about miserable conditions." His first concern is to rescue people from the miserable condition of hell. His second concern is to rescue sinning believers from being out of fellowship with Him. Lastly, His concern is the physical suffering of His creatures; He will often allow and impose physical suffering to bring a lost man to salvation or to restore fallen believers back to fellowship with Him.

   The question we must ask ourselves is "Do my priorities match God's priorities?" Think about your own situation. Do the concerns that plague you match the concerns God has? Are you more interested in physical relief and pleasure than you are spiritual growth? Do you have enough concern about the lost state of men to put yourself in the often "uncomfortable" situation of speaking to the unsaved about their eternal destiny?

   In the blanks below, rate your priorities based upon your actions and concerns within the past several months. Rate yourself as follows:

   1 = Never   2 = Sometimes   3 = Often   4 = Always

   ____ I am concerned about the lost estate of people around me, and I get very involved giving them the gospel in order to see them rescued from their miserable destiny.

   ____ I am concerned about my own spiritual condition and that of other believers around me when I see that I/we are out of fellowship with God, and I get very involved trying to rescue myself/them from the miserable condition of estrangement from God.

   ____ I am concerned about my own physical pain and that of others around me, and I get very involved trying to relieve that suffering.

After you have rated yourself on these three issues, what changes—if any—need to be made in your outlook on life?

2. Read Jeremiah 29:11 and Matthew 11:28–30. What do these passages tell you about the disposition of our God to rescue us from our "miserable conditions"?

3. What effect should the truth of these passages have upon your soul?

Chapter Nine

BEHOLDING THE GOD OF FAITHFULNESS

This I recall to my mind, therefore have I hope. It is of the Lord's mercies that we are not consumed, because his compassions fail not. They are new every morning: great is thy faithfulness. The Lord is my portion, saith my soul; therefore will I hope in him. The Lord is good unto them that wait for him, to the soul that seeketh him. It is good that a man should both hope and quietly wait for the salvation of the Lord. (Lamentations 3:21–26)

When my wife and I finished college, we thought God might be directing us to a foreign mission field. Through various means He demonstrated that He wanted us rather to minister long-term at Bob Jones University. During those days of missionary preparation, however, I was able to get a private pilot's license, thinking that God would use the skill on the mission field. Though I have not used the training for ministry—or pleasure—I did learn many lessons from flying that apply to Christian living. One comes to mind when I consider this topic of faithfulness.

Ten hours or so into my flight training my instructor was coaching me through my first landing and take-off from a grass strip in Union, South Carolina. Once we landed, my next objective was to take off from the short field. I taxied to the end of the field and was instructed to run the engine of the Cessna 150 to its maximum revolutions while holding both feet on the brakes at the start of the grass runway. At peak rpm I released the brakes, and the single-engine plane jolted forward, gaining enough speed in the short grass to take off and clear the trees at the end of the runway.

As I banked left steering to my next heading, I looked out my side window to the left to see the treetops merely a few feet below. Once I was on the right heading for my trip back to Greenville, I began checking the chart in my lap for recognizable landmarks—roads, rivers, power lines, water towers, and so forth. I located a couple of markers immediately after takeoff, but after several minutes on the heading nothing I was seeing matched what the chart said I should be seeing. I quickly took my bearings from two VORs (this was before general aviation used global positioning satellite units) and found that I was several miles off course. I calculated what my new heading should be and pointed the plane in that direction.

Again, within a few minutes I was seemingly off course. I repeated my calibrations and reset my course for the corrected heading. To my embarrassment, within minutes I was lost again. My instructor seemed to be enjoying my quandary and finally with a chuckle told me what he had done in order to teach me a valuable lesson.

While our plane had a magnetic compass attached where most automobiles have a rear view mirror, it is useful for only general directions since it bounces around so much in the aircraft. Navigation is done using a DG (directional gyroscope). Since the instrument uses a gyroscope, it gives a very steady heading. Its only drawback is that it drifts by precession. That means that over time the needle will have drifted several degrees from the true heading. That is not a problem in the short flights I was doing but could be disastrous over longer journeys.

In order to guarantee that the DG was accurate, a pilot is to always reset the instrument to the runway heading just before takeoff. Every runway points to a compass heading that is painted in large letters at the beginning of the runway. A pilot knows that if he has taxied to the end of a runway painted with 36 that his plane is pointed at a heading of 360 degrees on the compass. He is to reach over and turn his DG needle to 360, calibrating it to a true known heading.

I had been failing to do this, and my instructor noticed my neglect. He had reminded me a couple of times, but in the flurry of activity just before takeoff I was forgetting to calibrate my DG. On this takeoff while I was banking left and looking out my side window, he had reached over and set my DG off course by about 20 degrees. No matter what heading I turned to, it was 20 degrees off course, and it wasn't long before

I was lost. The lesson was so embarrassing that I never forgot to reset my DG ever again.

What was Israel's problem? They forgot the Lord their God; they did not remember His works. *Their hearts drifted from what they knew to be true about God.* They got off course, and it brought about their captivity and eventual dispersement throughout the Gentile world.

This is why it is so important for us to daily be in our Bible seeking to know God. This is why it is crucial for us to regularly attend a Bible-preaching church where we can hear the exposition of God's Word. This is why we must "exhort one another . . . lest any of you be hardened through the deceitfulness of sin" (Hebrews 3:13).

Our hearts tend to drift like directional gyros, and if they are not reset according to an unchangeable standard—the Scriptures—we will soon be off course in our thinking and acting. One area that we are particularly prone to drift in our thinking is the faithfulness of God. When things do not go the way we would like, we tend to think that God's love has failed or that He was short on wisdom when He let something happen that makes life difficult. It is amazing how quickly we charge God with some sort of deficiency when life gets rough. We need to take a good look at the faithfulness of our God if our souls are to be quiet.

WHAT DOES IT MEAN THAT GOD IS FAITHFUL?

God's faithfulness is a subset of a larger attribute of God—His immutability, or His unchangeableness. This is the basis for the statements you saw earlier (i.e., God is always good—ALWAYS!). Political climates, moods, weather, stock markets, churches, relationships, health, and fashions all change, but God never changes.

The prophet Jeremiah proclaims, "[Thy mercies] are new every morning; great is thy faithfulness" (Lamentations 3:23). This is a far cry from the experience of some who seem to have as their life verse a perversion of this passage: "Their crises are new every morning; great are their calamities." Their emotional stability is lost as they jump from heading to heading on their course of life.

But God says, "I intend for you to wake up every morning aware of My faithfulness. I do not change." Because of God's unchangeableness you and I can respond to life's ups and downs with steady confidence that

God is working out these circumstances for our good and for His glory (Romans 8:28–29). Listen to the Scripture's testimony about God's faithfulness.

> Know therefore that the Lord thy God, he is God, the faithful God, which keepeth covenant and mercy with them that love him and keep his commandments to a thousand generations. (Deuteronomy 7:9)

> Of old hast thou laid the foundation of the earth: and the heavens are the work of thy hands. They shall perish, but thou shalt endure: yea, all of them shall wax old like a garment; as a vesture shalt thou change them, and they shall be changed: but thou art the same, and thy years shall have no end. (Psalm 102:25–27)

> God is not a man, that he should lie; neither the son of man, that he should repent: hath he said, and shall he not do it? or hath he spoken, and shall he not make it good? (Numbers 23:19)

> For I am the Lord, I change not. (Malachi 3:6)

> Every good gift and every perfect gift is from above, and cometh down from the Father of lights, with whom is no variableness, neither shadow of turning. (James 1:17)

Celestial bodies cast varying shadows as they move around the sun, and the moon waxes and wanes, but God is always the same.

That God is faithful means that He finishes what He starts and pays for what He orders. He never leaves us. He never forsakes us. He is always present with us. He always forgives us. He always directs us. He always provides a way to escape temptation.

To change in any way would mean that God would have to change for the better, but He is already perfect. Or He would have to change for the worse, but that too is not possible since He is perfection.

Furthermore, everything about God exists in perfect harmony. He doesn't have to "work on" anything in His life. He never runs low on patience—or love—or wisdom—or power. He doesn't have to beef up His mercy to compensate for His justice.

Perfect attributes don't fight each other. He doesn't have internal battles with His personal characteristics. He is perfect in every way and never changes.

WHAT MAKES GOD SO UNCHANGEABLE?

At first you may think this is a bit heavy, but stay with me. You might have to stretch some mental muscles, but that's OK.

First of all, God is unchangeable because He is the Self-Existent One. That means that no one made God and no one can influence Him to contradict Himself in any way. No one can make Him do anything against His will.

We, on the other hand, change with the slightest cause. Our moods and opinions change with the weather, a stain on our clothes, a low score on a test, a loss of a ball game, or a cross look from a friend. It doesn't take much to change us.

The hymn "Immortal, Invisible" catches this contrast: "We blossom and flourish as leaves on the tree; And wither and perish, but naught changeth Thee!"[1]

When God told Moses to go to Egypt and command Pharaoh to release the Hebrew people from captivity, Moses said,

> Behold, when I come unto the children of Israel, and shall say unto them, The God of your fathers hath sent me unto you; and they shall say to me, What is his name? what shall I say unto them? And God said unto Moses, I AM THAT I AM: and he said, Thus shalt thou say unto the children of Israel, I AM hath sent me unto you. (Exodus 3:13–14)

In essence, God said to Moses, "Tell them that The-Never-Changing-One sent you. Tell them that the One-Who-Promised-a-Seed-and-a-Land-to-Abraham sent you—the Changeless One. I am what I have been; I am what I am; and I am what I shall be."

God is unchangeable because He is the Self-Existent One. He is free from any cause outside Himself that would change Him in any way.

Secondly, God is unchangeable because He is the Infinite One. He is free from all limitations. Nothing He purposes needs to be revised, rethought, or renegotiated because of some obstacle or new information. He has no need to change anything.

You and I often review something we did and say, "I wish I had thought of . . ." or "If I could do that over again, I would. . . ." Because we are imperfect and finite, we often need to change plans. We cannot know everything ahead of time or foresee what is coming. God does not have that limitation with His infinite knowledge, wisdom, and power.

It is because of His infinite perfections that He does not have to send revisions or additions to the Bible. He won't be sending us *Bible II* or *The Return of the Bible*. There is no need for a sequel. When He speaks, He says all He needs to say the first time.

Again, a hymn writer captured these truths and set them in beautiful verse and melody.

> Who spread out the clouds before Him? Who fashioned the
> earth with His hands?
> Who created the starry host, and formed the earth with
> His command?
> Who scatters lightning before Him, commands the rain
> and snow to fall?
> Who makes the nations tremble? Who is Lord over all?
> He is almighty, unchangeable God.
> King of kings, Lord of Lords, robed in majesty.
> He rules and reigns for all eternity.
> Almighty, unchangeable God.[2]

He is unlimited—infinite—in every way and, therefore, cannot change! What great stability this truth should bring to our troubled minds!

WHY DOES IT MATTER THAT GOD IS FAITHFUL?

First, without a clear view of God's faithfulness you will not have a very stable testimony for God. *God's faithfulness fuels our faithfulness.*

You will be plagued by sins you cannot overcome if you do not believe that God is faithful. Note the following passages.

> There hath no temptation taken you but such as is common to man: but God is faithful, who will not suffer you to be tempted above that ye are able; but will with the temptation also make a way to escape, that ye may be able to bear it. (1 Corinthians 10:13)

> Faithful is he that calleth you, who also will do it. (1 Thessalonians 5:24)

> But the Lord is faithful, who shall stablish you, and keep you from evil. (2 Thessalonians 3:3)

These promises regarding our growth in holiness are based upon the faithfulness of God to us. This is what prompted the hymn writer to say,*

> Pardon for sin and a peace that endureth,
> Thy own dear presence to cheer and to guide:
> Strength for today and bright hope for tomorrow.
> [These are] blessings all mine, with ten thousand beside.³

You may be unsure of your salvation and of the forgiveness of your sins if you do not believe that God is faithful.

> If we confess our sins, he is faithful and just to forgive us our sins, and to cleanse us from all unrighteousness. (1 John 1:9)

You can be easily discouraged by loneliness if you do not believe that God is faithful.

> I will never leave thee, nor forsake thee. (Hebrews 13:5)

Do you remember the words of the hymn "What a Friend We Have in Jesus?"

> Can we find a friend so faithful
> Who will all our sorrows share?
> Jesus knows our every weakness,
> Take it to the Lord in prayer.⁴

He is a faithful friend, and though it is nice to have other friends, we truly need no other.

You can easily be discouraged by your own failures if you do not believe that God is faithful.

> If we believe not, yet he abideth faithful: he cannot deny [contradict] himself. (2 Timothy 2:13)

We can become distressed when we don't come through for ourselves or for others. We can't seem to be everything others want us to be. We can't be as consistent as we would like to think. Being mortal and fallen we have many inadequacies. When we see our failures, we often become discouraged because our trust is in ourselves—and we let ourselves down. God often allows that so we can see that our trust needs

---

*Taken from "Great Is Thy Faithfulness" by Thomas Chisholm © 1923. Ren. 1951 Hope Publishing Co., Carol Stream, IL 60188, www.hopepublishing.com. All rights reserved. Used by permission.

to be in Someone Who is truly faithful; our confidence needs to be in Him.

You can be tortured by fear of what is going to happen if you do not believe that God is faithful.

> The Lord shall preserve thy going out and thy coming in from this time forth and even for evermore. (Psalm 121:8)

God knows the future. He knows how much we can take, and He knows exactly what we need. His faithfulness gives us confidence that He is ever watching over us for our good and for His own glory.

Not only will you have little testimony for God if you do not have a clear view of God's faithfulness, but without a clear view of God's faithfulness, you will have little trust in God. God's faithfulness not only fuels our faithfulness, as we have just seen, but *His faithfulness fuels our faith*. You cannot build a stable life while trying to believe in a God you see as unpredictable and scary to you.

When I was in the ninth grade, I took a couple of semesters of Latin. One of our projects was to read the *Aeneid* by Homer (in English). I was struck with how unpredictable and capricious the gods were. A mortal on the earth never knew if the gods were going to rain on his crops or burn them. He never knew where he stood with the gods.

Once a god got involved in a person's life, the person's life could become very complicated very quickly. In fact, most mortals were quite content to not involve the gods in their lives at all, unless they needed them for some great feat or deliverance. The gods were everything but faithful. They were not faithful to their own spouses. They were not faithful to their children. They were not faithful to their subjects. They lived entirely for the gratification of their own skewed desires.

The true God of heaven—the God of the Bible—is always entirely predictable. He never acts in any way inconsistent with His nature. He is always loving, always merciful, always wise, and so forth. It is this "always-ness" of His nature that makes Him faithful, and therefore trustworthy and predictable.

God's promises will have little impact upon you if you do not believe that He is faithful.

> [Abraham] staggered not at the promise of God through unbelief;
> but was strong in faith, giving glory to God; And being fully per-
> suaded that, what he had promised, he was able also to perform.
> (Romans 4:20–21)

When I was a boy, my parents left the farm to enter full-time Christian work in a faith-based children's ministry. They had raised the necessary monthly support, but sadly, only about half of it ever came in. Those were difficult times for us. Dad was gone much of the time traveling our state holding training classes and children's rallies. I know it was hard for him to leave knowing that his wife and three boys were at home with very little money to live.

I was sometimes resentful that I didn't have the things that other kids my age seemed to have, but I never doubted that we would have what we *needed*. You see, I had seen God answer my parents' prayers over and over again. I had seen Him provide groceries for us on more than one occasion when there was not a single bit of food left in the house. I had seen Him provide clothing—though hand-me-downs—for us boys as we outgrew our pants and shirts. I had watched my parents trust a faithful God, and I never saw them disappointed in His provisions.

My parents "staggered not at the promise of God through unbelief." They knew God to be faithful. They claimed His promises, and He always provided. God's faithfulness fueled their faith—and mine—as I watched them trust God.

Your prayer life will have little impact upon anything if you do not believe that God is faithful.

None of us will call upon someone we don't believe can help us. We simply won't pray. You and I must meditate upon the faithfulness of God!

HE IS FAITHFUL THAT HAS PROMISED

A couple of years ago at Christmas I decided to study the Old Testament prophecies about the coming Messiah. I wanted to see afresh what God had promised and watch history unfold to faithfully fulfill His Word.

I saw the faithful God in Genesis 1, after the fall of Adam and Eve into sin and death, promise that one day a descendent of the woman would crush the serpent's head.

I saw in Exodus the faithful God promise to spare the firstborn sons of the Israelites in Egypt when He saw the blood of the Passover lamb on the doorposts.

I saw the faithful God promise a suffering Savior in Isaiah 53—One Who would be "wounded for our transgressions."

I saw the faithful God promise a young, Jewish virgin that she would bear the Messiah, and I saw the faithful God fulfill His promise to an old Jewish priest named Simeon, who held the Messiah, lifted up his eyes to heaven, and said,

> Mine eyes have seen thy salvation . . . a light to lighten the Gentiles. (Luke 2:30–32)

I rejoiced when I contemplated the fact that those Gentiles included me!

I saw the faithful God provide His own Lamb, Who lived a perfect life and thereby qualified to be a sinless atoning sacrifice for me as I saw the earthly ministry of Jesus unfold and then end in His crucifixion and resurrection.

And finally, "I saw heaven opened, and behold a white horse; and he that sat upon him was called *Faithful* and True" (Revelation 19:11, emphasis mine). Here is the ultimate, triumphal entry of the Messiah!

This is our God, folks. This is The Faithful One! I rejoiced with the hymn writer Isaac Watts, who said,

> Before the hills in order stood,
> Or earth received her frame,
> From everlasting Thou art God,
> Through endless years the same.[5]

He never changes; He is The Faithful God!

My soul—and yours—can rest because *God's faithfulness is more than enough for us.*

Take Time to Reflect

1. In what ways are you plagued by sins you cannot overcome? How often and to what extent do you have doubts about your salvation or about God's forgiveness of your sins?

2. Are you often plagued by loneliness and to what degree?

3. How discouraged do you become at your own failures? How tortured are you by fears of what might happen in your life?

4. What part does reviewing and claiming the promises of God play in the way you handle the challenges of life?

5. What part does prayer play in the way you handle the challenges of life?

Chapter Ten

BEHOLDING THE GOD OF POWER

Thine, O Lord, is the greatness, and the power, and the glory, and the victory, and the majesty: for all that is in the heaven and in the earth is thine; thine is the kingdom, O Lord, and thou art exalted as head above all. Both riches and honour come of thee, and thou reignest over all; and in thine hand is power and might; and in thine hand it is to make great, and to give strength unto all. Now therefore, our God, we thank thee, and praise they glorious name. (1 Chronicles 29:11–13)

In 1981 Rabbi Harold Kushner published a best-selling book entitled *When Bad Things Happen to Good People*. He attempted to make sense out of a family tragedy. He concluded that either God was good but not powerful enough to keep bad things from happening, or He was powerful but not good enough to intervene.

He sided with the opinion that God was indeed good, but His power was defective. He was particularly troubled about what happened to Job. He concluded that although God wants the righteous to live happy and peaceful lives, sometimes He just can't prevent calamity from taking over.

What a contrast Kushner's misinformed view is to the view of Stephen Charnock.

> The power of God is that ability and strength whereby He can bring to pass whatsoever He pleases, whatsoever His infinite wisdom may direct, and whatsoever the infinite purity of His will may resolve. . . . As holiness is the beauty of all God's attributes, so power is that which gives life and action to all the perfections of the Divine nature. How vain would be the eternal counsels, if power did not step in to execute them. Without

power His mercy would be but feeble pity, His promises empty sound, His threatening a mere scarecrow. God's power is like Himself: infinite, eternal, incomprehensible; it can neither be checked, restrained, nor frustrated by the creature.[1]

ABSOLUTE MIGHT

That God has all power means that He possesses absolute might. The New Testament word for this power is *dunamis*, which refers to the "power, ability, physical or moral, as residing in a person or thing."[2] When we speak of God's almighty power, we often use the term *omnipotence*. That means that "God is able to do whatever He wills in the way He wills it."[3]

One summer while I was in college, I was impressed with the "able" passages of the New Testament. I meditated often upon the truths in the following verses. They greatly increased my confidence in God's power.

> God is *able* to make all grace abound toward you; that ye, always having all sufficiency in all things, may abound to every good work. (2 Corinthians 9:8, emphasis mine)

> Now unto him that is *able* to do exceeding abundantly above all that we ask or think, according to the power that worketh in us. (Ephesians 3:20, emphasis mine)

> [Abraham] staggered not at the promise of God through unbelief; but was strong in faith, giving glory to God; And being fully persuaded that, what he had promised, he was *able* also to perform. (Romans 4:20–21, emphasis mine)

> For I know whom I have believed, and am persuaded that he is *able* to keep that which I have committed unto him against that day. (2 Timothy 1:12, emphasis mine)

> Wherefore he is *able* also to save them to the uttermost that come unto God by him, seeing he ever liveth to make intercession for them. (Hebrews 7:25, emphasis mine)

> Now unto him that is *able* to keep you from falling, and to present you faultless before the presence of his glory with exceeding joy. (Jude 24, emphasis mine)

These statements cover a wide range of needs for which we can depend upon God because He is able. He has the absolute might to carry out everything He wills.

HIS POWER IN CREATION

Isaiah 40 is a wonderful chapter declaring the power of God in creation. Isaiah asks in verse 12,

> Who hath measured the waters in the hollow of his hand, and meted out heaven with the span, and comprehended the dust of the earth in a measure, and weighed the mountains in scales, and the hills in a balance?

Only a powerful God could do all this. He asks us to consider the heavens as well in verse 26.

> Lift up your eyes on high, and behold who hath created these [stars], that bringeth out their host by number: he calleth them all by names by the greatness of his might, for that he is strong in power; not one faileth.

A. W. Tozer when commenting on this passage says,

> Now this passage is probably the most daring flight of imagination ever made by the human mind. We have here in Isaiah that which is vaster and more awesome than anything that ever came out of the mind of Shakespeare. It is the thought of the great God, the Shepherd of the universe, moving through His universe, with its billions and trillions of light years, with its worlds so big that our whole solar system would look like a grain of sand in comparison. And God stands out yonder and calls all of these millions of worlds as His sheep; He calls them all by name and leads them across the vast sky.

> I'd say this is the highest thought I know of, in the Bible or out. And God does this "by the greatness of his might, for that he is strong in power; not one faileth" (40:26). Just as a shepherd keeps all his sheep and not one is lost, so God keeps all His universe. Men point their tiny little glasses at the stars and talk learnedly, but they've just been counting God's sheep, nothing more. God is running His universe.[4]

My wife and I have ministered to the dear believers on the islands of Hawaii over the years. I remember the first time my host took us to the top of Diamond Head on Oahu. I am from the Midwest and had never spent much time around the ocean. From the perspective of that extinct volcanic rim I could see nothing except ocean.

The tide was out and my host pointed to where it would come when it was in. I tried to think about how much water God had to move from one place to the other just to bring the tide in. My children were young at that time, and I remembered how much work it was to move their two-ring inflatable swimming pool from one place in the backyard to another in order to prevent it from killing the grass. I had to tug and pull just to move a few gallons of water. Here, before my eyes, God was moving the entire Pacific Ocean in and out without any effort at all! What amazing power!

I had just seen a brief news clip about how a movie director had simulated a storm at sea for an upcoming movie. The crew had built a pond and installed some enormous hydraulically operated "paddles" that moved back and forth to create immense waves in the pond. I looked over the Honolulu harbor and realized that all God had to do was say the word, and He could whip up a hurricane of immense proportion. This is power!

In Genesis 1 all God had to say was "Let there be light" and "there was light" (1:3). This is astonishing power! The creation shows the enormous power of our great Creator God. He is able!

HIS POWER IN PRESERVATION

God's preserving power is called His providence. The behavior of the weather is not just a matter of low and high pressure systems. It is the product of the moment by moment superintendence of God. One author has put it this way:

> Christ is the originator and upholder of the universe. . . . In him it consists, or holds together, from hour to hour. The steady will of Christ constitutes the law of the universe and makes it a cosmos instead of chaos, just as His will brought it into being in the beginning.[5]

Incidentally, that is why complaints against the weather are complaints against God Himself—He purposefully controls it just as it is happening. This is also why natural "disasters" are called "acts of God."

The same is true for birth defects, cancer, disabilities, accidents, disease, and even death. These, along with all the good things that happen in life, are superintended by God, and He is willing to take full responsibility for them all. He has the wisdom to know what is best, the loving heart to will what is best, and the power to carry it out.

HIS POWER IN GOVERNMENT

Every president, every congressman, every senator, every governor, every foreign prime minister, every tyrant, and every terrorist is under the government of God. Witness in the Bible how God used men such as Pharaoh, Nebuchadnezzar, Belteshazzar, Cyrus, Artexerxes, and Herod to accomplish His plans. These men thought they were working out their own plans. God was using their plans to do His will in the earth.

My freshman year of college when God was drawing me to Himself, He showed me from Romans 13:1–2 that my responses to my authorities revealed my response to God Himself. Paul said,

> Let every soul be subject unto the higher [authorities]. For there is no [authority] but of God: the powers that be [the authorities that exist] are ordained of God. Whosoever therefore resisteth the [authority], resisteth the ordinance of God: and they that resist shall receive to themselves [judgment].

I was frustrated with some of the restraints. I couldn't do what I wanted; I couldn't go out when I wanted to go out. It occurred to me that God knew those restrictions when He called me to BJU. He didn't wake up from an afternoon nap one day, find me at BJU, and then worry about how I was going to make it with my free-spirited heart. He knew what BJU was doing. He knew what I needed, and He superintended my life so that I ended up there. Those authorities were His choice for me, and I needed to get with *His* program and stop demanding my own way. Those were the thoughts He brought to bear upon my mind as I meditated upon Romans 13:1–2.

We have to be very careful today. Like Pharisees we like to narrow biblical statements so far down that they don't apply to us. It is true that God *ordained* only three authorities—the home, the state, and the church. That does not mean those are the only *legitimate* authorities. The most obvious biblical example is slavery. None of us would say that God *ordained* slavery, but nonetheless, He dictated how believing slaves should obey their masters (Ephesians 6:5–8; Colossians 3:22–24; 1 Timothy 6:1–2; etc.). God does not permit His creatures to disobey any authority except under very narrowly defined exceptions outlined in the Bible.

The point is that we reveal much about our submission to God's authority by how we relate to the authorities He has placed in our lives: civil government, parents, church leaders, camp directors, husbands, employers, school officials, or proprietors of the businesses we frequent.

While these authorities often will reject the counsel of God and will use their power to advance their own ends, they cannot ultimately thwart the will of God. Consider the words of Alexander Carson.

> Why does folly often prevail over wisdom in the counsels of princes, and in the houses of legislators? God has appointed the rejection of good counsel in order to bring on nations that vengeance that their crimes call down from heaven. God rules the world by Providence, not by miracle. See that grave senator. He rises and pours forth wisdom. But if God has determined to punish the nation, some prating secularist will impose his sophism on the most sagacious assembly.[6]

HIS ABSOLUTE RIGHT

That God has all power also means that He possesses absolute right. The New Testament word for this concept is *exousia*. It "denotes freedom of action, right to act; used of God, it is absolute, unrestricted; used of men, authority is delegated."[7]

God's control is absolute

"If there is a single event in all of the universe that can occur outside of God's sovereign control, then we cannot trust Him."[8] We might ask why that is so. Others have failed us, and we still trust them. Why should it be any different with God? The reason is that no one else has claimed to have everything under control. If God is untrustworthy at any point, how do we know in what other areas He is untrustworthy?

The psalmist assures us that nothing escapes God's control. David said, "The Lord hath prepared his throne in the heavens; and his kingdom ruleth over all" (Psalm 103:19). What a comforting truth this is. The statement "his kingdom ruleth over all" is far-reaching and absolute. We need not fear that anyone or anything can happen without His direct involvement.

God's control is not always apparent

"He permits, for reasons known only to Himself, people to act contrary to and in defiance of His revealed will. But He never permits them to act contrary to His sovereign will."[9] Criminals can break into our homes and harm us, politicians with freedom-destroying policies can be elected to office, loved ones may turn against us, or factories may shut down because of mismanagement or fraud. None of these evils means that God is not in control. Consider again what the Scriptures have to say to us about the sovereignty—the reign—of our great God.

> Thine, O Lord is the greatness, and the power, and the glory, and the victory, and the majesty: for all that is in the heaven and in the earth is thine; thine is the kingdom, O Lord, and thou art exalted as head above all. Both riches and honour come of thee, and thou reignest over all; and in thine hand is power and might; and in thine hand it is to make great, and to give strength unto all. (1 Chronicles 29:11–12)

> Thou, even thou, art Lord alone; thou hast made heaven, the heaven of heavens, with all their host, the earth, and all things that are therein, the seas, and all that is therein, and thou preservest them all; and the host of heaven worshippeth thee. (Nehemiah 9:6)

> The Lord hath prepared his throne in the heavens; and his kingdom ruleth over all. (Psalm 103:19)

> And I heard as it were the voice of a great multitude, and as the voice of many waters, and as the voice of mighty thunderings, saying, Alleluia: for the Lord God omnipotent reigneth. (Revelation 19:6)

These truths about God's absolute might and right are the truths that stabilized Abraham, Moses, Esther, Ruth, the prophets, godly kings, apostles, the persecuted church, and the heroes of the faith in Hebrews 11.

Most notably these truths sustained Joseph (Genesis 37–50). He was a teenager from a dysfunctional family (four competing mothers, ten brothers who couldn't stand him, a doting father, and a spoiled sister) who was sold into slavery by envious brothers.

Many decisions were made for him by his brothers' single decision. He lived in a land he didn't choose, spoke a language that wasn't his, and worked at a job, ate food, and wore clothes that someone else picked. His freedoms were taken away and his quality of life greatly denigrated, yet he was remarkably stable and demonstrated unusual initiative when seeking the welfare of his slave master. What lies behind this kind of stability? Joseph himself told us in Genesis 50:20 (the Romans 8:28 of the Old Testament).

When seeking reconciliation with his brothers for their grievous evil against him, Joseph showed his steadfast confidence in the involvement of a sovereign God in his life. He told his brothers, "Ye thought evil against me; but God meant it unto good."

He trusted the promises of God that one day his family would bow to him, and he trusted the power of God to bring it to pass as He had promised.

Why did Joseph's soul rest? Why was he not agitated and irritated at every reversal of life? Why was his soul quiet? What drained the toxins of anxiety, anger, and despair out of his heart? It was the knowledge of his omnipotent God! You and I, too, can rest because *God's power is more than enough for us.*

Take Time to Reflect

1. Describe some situations in your life when it seemed that God was not in control. Also, describe how you responded to those situations.

2. How might you have responded differently to the above situations had you seen clearly at the time that God is powerful?

3. Read Genesis 37 and 50:14–22. The story of Joseph would have turned out differently had Joseph not believed in God's ability to perform His promises to him. How might the story be different if Joseph had been bitter at his brothers?

Chapter Eleven

BEHOLDING THE GOD OF WISDOM

O the depth of the riches both of the wisdom and knowledge of God! how unsearchable are his judgments, and his ways past finding out! (Romans 11:33)

HOW MUCH DOES GOD KNOW?

We must begin this chapter with a look at God's knowledge, since His wisdom is based upon His knowledge. You can't be wise unless you know something. Listen to what one commentator has said about the wisdom of God.

> Great is our Lord, and of great power: his understanding is infinite (Psalm 147:5). God knows everything that has happened in every part of His vast domain. Furthermore, He is thoroughly acquainted with everything that is now transpiring throughout the entire universe. Finally, He is also perfectly cognizant of every event from the least to the greatest that ever will happen. God's knowledge of the future is as complete as His knowledge of the past and the present because the future depends entirely upon His actions. Were it possible for something to occur apart from either the direct agency or permission of God, then that something would be independent of Him, and He would at once cease to be Supreme.[1]

Let's look more specifically at the nature of His knowledge.

God's knowledge is infinite

You and I face situations continually where we run out of wisdom. We don't know what to do next. We exhaust all the options we can think of. God never has that problem. Every one of His powers—including His knowledge—is limitless. He is omniscient—all-knowing.

David, Daniel, and Ezekiel were very much aware of God's total knowledge of everything in their lives.

> O Lord, thou hast searched me, and known me. Thou knowest my downsitting and mine uprising, thou understandest my thought afar off. Thou compassest my path and my lying down, and art acquainted with all my ways. For there is not a word in my tongue, but, lo, O Lord, thou knowest it altogether. Thou hast beset me behind and before, and laid thine hand upon me. Such knowledge is too wonderful for me; it is high, I cannot attain unto it. (Psalm 139:1–6)
>
> He knoweth what is in the darkness. (Daniel 2:22)
>
> I know the things that come into your mind, every one of them. (Ezekiel 11:5)

Of course, this comprehensive knowledge that God possesses can be quite comforting, or it can be quite disturbing depending upon what you and I are doing or thinking at the moment.

God's knowledge is intuitive

Let's consider also that because God's knowledge is infinite; it is therefore intuitive. That means that God does not learn anything. He has no need to learn anything. As someone once asked, "Did it ever occur to you that nothing ever occurs to God?" He doesn't have a new idea. He knows everything *actual*, everything *possible*, and everything *imaginable*. The writer to the Hebrews declared, "Neither is there any creature that is not manifest [revealed] in his sight: but all things are naked and opened unto the eyes of him with whom we have to do" (Hebrews 4:13).

God not only never learns anything because He already knows it all, but He never deliberates about anything. He never ponders or agonizes or wonders about something. He intuitively knows what is the best thing to do because all the facts are at His disposal all the time.

God's knowledge is infallible

Because God's knowledge is infinite, it is also infallible. God never gets wrong information. He doesn't have to send angels on errands to search the heavenly databanks for the pertinent facts and then find out that they missed some crucial piece of information. The apostle James declared at the Jerusalem council, "Known unto God are all His works from the beginning" (Acts 15:18). He doesn't have to rely upon anyone else to uncover the facts since He personally knows everything there is to know.

Don't miss the significance of these truths! If God knows all things, never gets wrong information, and is, therefore, infallible, these have enormous implications for us when He tells us in the Scriptures how to think about something or what to do about something. We can't go wrong listening to and obeying what He says. His is the only fully accurate view of reality.

The believer's responses

The proper responses to this kind of superior knowledge are twofold. The first is *wonder*. Notice what David says about God's infinite knowledge in Psalm 139:6.

> Such knowledge is too wonderful [awesome] for me; it is high, I cannot attain unto it.

David said this knowledge caused him to be "full of wonder"—wonderful. Today, we would say it is "awesome"; it fills the observer with awe—even with fear and trembling.

We get a small taste of this awe anytime we contemplate the intricacies and magnitude of the natural creation. Whether a person is looking at the expanse of the universe or the complexities of the human genome, a thinking person is awed with the level of intelligence that brought these materials into existence, outfitted them with their various properties, and created the physical laws under which they thrive and function.

I think this is one of the reasons that God made the cosmos so vast and locked its secrets into particles and waves that are invisible to the human eye. He intended for the viewers of His works to be lost in wonder and humbled. Nature gives us a taste of the infinite—though it is not truly infinite.

Stop to think about the difficulty of creating a working and thriving universe out of nothing. If that were my task, I wouldn't know where to start. I can't even recall the elements of the periodic table, let alone prescribe their properties so that they function together in harmony and usefulness. This is a job that requires knowledge and wisdom far beyond what you and I can even imagine; we certainly couldn't make it happen!

God used the vastness and the order of the created universe to quiet Job's troubled soul about the mysteries of his life (Job 38–42). When he was forced to contemplate God's wisdom in creating and maintaining the physical world around him, Job was also forced to bow in humility to the wisdom that prescribed his "calamities."

Wonder naturally leads to *worship*—the second response to God's superior knowledge and wisdom. In Revelation 15 the blood-washed saints who have gone before us, when contemplating all the acts of God, praise His judgments—His decisions—and worship God. We, like Job, begin to question God's decisions when the problem drags on. But none of us on this earth has all the facts. Our knowledge is incomplete. In heaven, the saints see with clearer vision. Notice their response of worship at the infinitely wise decisions of God.

> And they sing the song of Moses the servant of God, and the song of the Lamb, saying, Great and marvellous are thy works, Lord God Almighty; just and true are thy ways, thou King of saints. Who shall not fear thee, O Lord, and glorify thy name? for thou only art holy: for all nations shall come and worship before thee; for thy judgments [decisions] are made manifest. (Revelation 15:3–4)

> And I heard the angel of the waters say, Thou art righteous, O Lord, which art, and wast, and shalt be, because thou hast judged thus. For they [the evil ones on the earth who have just been judged by God] have shed the blood of saints and prophets, and thou hast given them blood to drink; for they are worthy. And I heard another out of the altar say, Even so, Lord God Almighty, true and righteous are thy judgments [decisions]. (Revelation 16:5–7)

> And after these things I heard a great voice of much people in heaven, saying, Alleluia; salvation, and glory, and honour, and power, unto the Lord God: for true and righteous are his judgments [decisions]. (Revelation 19:1–2)

Someday when we have all the facts, we too will say, "We will glorify Your name because we see the evident wisdom of all Your decisions!"

God's knowledge is incomprehensible

God's knowledge is not only infinite, intuitive, and infallible but it is incomprehensible. It cannot be fully understood by finite, fallible minds like ours. We often cannot understand why something has happened or what good can come from it.

> As we watch tragic events unfolding, or more particularly as we experience adversity ourselves, we often are prone to ask God, "why?" The reason we ask is because we do not see any possible good to us or glory to God that can come from the particular adverse circumstances that have come upon us or our loved ones. But is not the wisdom of God—thus the glory of God—more eminently displayed in bringing good out of calamity than out of blessing?
>
> The wisdom of the chess player is displayed more in winning over a capable opponent than over a novice. The wisdom of the general is displayed more in defeating a superior army than in subduing an inferior one. Even more so, the wisdom of God is displayed more when He brings good to us and glory to Himself out of confusion and calamity rather than out of pleasant times.[2]

God assures us often in His Word that He will use everything for our good and for His glory. Sometimes I have heard people say that when someone is suffering you should not remind them of Romans 8:28. That is a serious mistake. The promises of God are meant to provide great comfort in times of need. We certainly should be careful about quipping, "Remember Romans 8:28," but we never want to remove it from the toolbox of God's promises. Think through it carefully.

> And we know that all things work together for good to them that love God, to them who are the called according to his purpose.

The truth of God's love skillfully—wisely—working every calamity and change into something that perfects His image in us should go a long way in quieting our noisy souls.

He promises similar good out of chastening if our hearts are tender toward Him.

> Now no chastening for the present seemeth to be joyous, but grievous: nevertheless afterward it yieldeth the peaceable fruit of righteousness unto them which are exercised thereby. (Hebrews 12:11)

The Scriptures remind us repeatedly that the ultimate good comes from something *after* we have patiently waited and *after* we have learned to turn our gaze upon God in the trial. God wisely sustains us in the trouble while He lovingly matures us through the trial. These truths may be the only "whys" we understand about our trials—the purpose of our growth in Christlikeness.

We are called rather to understand the "Who" behind our trials. We too often are seeking satisfaction from knowing what is going on and why. We must learn the contentment that comes from knowing only the Who behind them.

As we saw earlier, God quieted Job's noisy soul with a display of Who (Job 38–42), not an explanation of why. C. H. Spurgeon put it this way in a sermon on God's providence:

> Providence is wonderfully intricate. Ah! You want always to see through Providence, do you not? You never will, I assure you. You have not eyes good enough. You want to see what good that affliction was to you; you must believe it. You want to see how it can bring good to your soul; you may be enabled in a little time; but you can not see it now; you must believe it. Honor God by trusting Him.[3]

I remember a particularly teachable moment with my oldest daughter, Kirsten, when she was in the seventh grade. She wanted to attend a birthday party one of her friends was having for a classmate in the university snack shop after school one day. Junior high behavior is not typically welcomed by the university students, so we had instructed our children not to patronize the snack shop unless with an adult.

This was a special occasion, so I thought with a bit of forewarning the situation might be harmless. I asked who was attending and discovered that one particularly rowdy boy had been invited. I cautioned Kirsten that if he started acting up she should be prepared to leave so that she wasn't a part of any trouble that might come. She burst into tears and said for the first time that I could remember, "Daddy, you don't trust me!"

I wasn't expecting that response and thought a moment about how to reply. I asked her if at age twelve she was ready to drive our car to the grocery store for her mother. She replied she wasn't because she didn't know how to drive. I told her I was eager for the day when she would drive so that her mother wouldn't have to shuttle her and her sisters around so much but that I agreed she wasn't ready. She would need to take driver's training and then drive with me in the passenger side for some time before I would let her do it alone. Until then she would need some coaching.

I let her know that this situation was similar. She had never been in a situation quite like this one before, and she needed to be willing to take some coaching about what to do if problems arose. I then asked her if her mother or I had ever given her advice that didn't work. She replied that we never had. I asked her then, "Sweetie, if Dad is just trying to coach you so that you will know what to do, and if we haven't given you bad advice before, the real question is 'Why don't you trust Dad?'"

She again burst into tears, asked for my forgiveness, and we hugged and prayed together. (Incidentally, the party went without a hitch. Whew!)

The real question is even more penetrating when applied to our trust in God. Since He has never made any mistakes because He has full knowledge of all things, shouldn't we be willing to trust Him? His knowledge is infinite, infallible, and incomprehensible.

WHAT IS WISDOM?

It is commonly understood that wisdom is "knowing and choosing the best means to the best end." That statement has several critical components: knowing, choosing, best means, best end. We can fail to be wise by being ignorant of the best means and the best end (not "knowing") or by "knowing" the best means and best ends but not "choosing" it. That is the same as "hearing" but not "doing" (Matthew 7:24–27; James 1:21–25).

We must both "know" and "choose" what is the best means and the best end. But we must know what is the "best end" and the "best means" of attaining it.

> In addition to knowing all the relevant data on any subject, God selects ends with discernment and acts in harmony with His purposes of holy love. We may not always be able to see that events in our lives work together for a wise purpose, but we know that God chooses from among all the possible alternatives the best ends and means for achieving them. God not only chooses the right ends but also for the right reasons, the good of His creatures and thus His glory. . . . The divine omniscience is aware not only of what is, but also what ought to be [morally].[4]

Christian education, Christian parenting, Christian counseling—all aspects of Christian discipleship—are primarily about teaching wisdom (Christlikeness)—how to know and choose the best means to the best end. That requires some advice that is hard—or at least unwelcome—at the moment.

When I was ready for my first automobile in 1968, my dad let me buy a 1961 VW bug. The VW was a popular car during that time. Young people painted them wild colors and plastered them with peace signs and flowers. My bug was painted a factory industrial gray. It looked like something Hitler had produced for a staff car when he first started producing VWs.

I had visions of painting it lemon yellow with a faux black pebble grain finish on the roof to make it look like a convertible. My dad, being the wise mechanic that he was, had other priorities.

He reminded me of the "best end" of an automobile. He told me, "Son, a car isn't a status symbol or a means to make people stop and take notice of you. It is primarily a means of safe and reliable transportation." He then charged me with the responsibility to put new pads on the brakes and fix the leaks in two of the push rod tubes before I could spend one dollar on the externals.

Once the "best end" of safe and reliable transportation was clarified, it was obvious that the "best means" meant fixing mechanical problems. Cosmetics were not a "best means" to the "best end." Dad was a wise mechanic because he knew both the "best end" and the "best means." This is wisdom when applied to mechanics. It is how wisdom is demonstrated in any field.

Wisdom must choose based upon the knowledge of the facts. This is why wisdom in living requires much Bible study and meditation. Our hearts do not come preprogrammed to know the best means and best ends, nor do our hearts have the inclination to choose those means and ends when they go against our desires of the moment.

Since we are not predisposed or preprogrammed to know these things, we must get them from somewhere outside ourselves. Proverbs instructs us that the only place we can get wisdom is from God Himself and from people who point us to God.

> For the *Lord* giveth wisdom: out of *his* mouth cometh knowledge and understanding. (Proverbs 2:6, emphasis mine)

If you hang around people of the world and listen to them, you can become worldly-wise. If you hang around the streets, you can become streetwise. You can become spiritually wise only by "hanging around" God. Proverbs 1–4 is strikingly clear about this. You can have "the knowledge of God," which is the basis for wise decision-making only by seeking, contemplating, and embracing the words of the living God. The Scriptures are the only place you will get the right facts about life and about godliness.

Wisdom not only *knows* what is the best means to the best end but *chooses* those means and ends. I could have the facts right that the best end of an automobile is safe and reliable transportation but not choose to make decisions in light of that knowledge.

The best end of any choice we make must be our Christlikeness and God's glory. This is why many believers will never make the right decisions in the areas of so-called Christian liberty. They are not concerned first and foremost about the moral and ethical impact of their decisions upon their likeness to Christ. They have forgotten, or have chosen to ignore, the best end of all things—the glory of God.

Paul said of our relationship to God that "in him we live, and move, and have our being" (Acts 17:28). God is the "context" of our existence. We must know that and choose in light of that. We will have the wrong values if we ignore our context. Let me illustrate how our context determines our values.

I studied South Dakota history in sixth grade. During the gold rush that took place in the 1800s people headed west across the continent in Conestoga wagons heavily loaded with their fine furniture and dishes handed down from generations before in Europe.

When they came halfway across South Dakota on their way west to Deadwood and Lead, where the gold was, they would encounter the Missouri River, which runs north to south dividing the entire state in half. The Missouri River is often very wide and usually rather shallow and normally would not be too dangerous to cross. However, by the time the fortune hunters had come this far, they had lost an ox or horse and were literally short on horsepower.

The meager teams couldn't pull the wagons across unless they were lightened up considerably. We learned that there were piles of goods left on the east side of the river: pump organs, ornate beddings and furniture, dining room suites, fancy trunks loaded with heirlooms, and so forth.

We might ask, "Were these things of no value to these families?" They weren't of value in this context. Surviving the journey and reaching the Black Hills were the "best end," and the "best means" now meant dumping things that had value back east—but not here.

If you ignore or reject the "best end" of Christlikeness and ignore the context of existence—God Himself—you will adopt the wrong values and choose the wrong means. You will fail, and your soul will be noisy. Christian reader, we must be wise! We must know our God; we must know His ways, then we must choose those ways for ourselves. Only then can we be wise.

I love the way A. W. Tozer has addressed this issue.

> With the goodness of God to desire our highest welfare, the wisdom of God to plan it, and the power of God to achieve it, what do we lack? Surely we are the most favored of all creatures.[5]

What contentment this should produce in our souls! God wants to make us wise. He desires to give us an understanding of His ways. He wants our ultimate good. Our souls can rest because God's wisdom is more than enough for us!

Take Time to Reflect

1. What do the following verses say about God's wisdom, and why should they cause your soul to rest?

   Psalm 147:5

   Psalm 136:1–6

   Daniel 2:22

   Hebrews 4:13

2. What events in your past or present tempt you to doubt the wisdom of God?

3. God has many wise purposes for the adversities we experience. According to the following sequence of verses in Psalm 119, what are the wise purposes for our adversity?

   Psalm 119:67

   Psalm 119:71

   Psalm 119:75

   Psalm 119:92

   Psalm 119:10

Chapter Twelve

KEEPING YOUR SOUL QUIET

As we saw in the first chapter, our souls will be quiet when we practice heeding the Master's call to "come unto Me" and to "learn of Me." That involves much time spent with the Master Himself in His Word being taught by His Spirit. I want us to look together at the components that go into a relationship with Christ that results in a quiet soul.

MAINTAINING A QUIET SOUL REQUIRES A SAVIOR

One of the first truths we discussed in chapter 1 of this book is that Jesus delights in saving us! We've seen that theme repeated throughout our study as we've contemplated various aspects of the nature of God. We have learned that He is a merciful God—wanting to rescue us from our miserable conditions. He is a loving God—wanting to give us what is in our best interest even at personal sacrifice to Himself. One thing should be clear to us: He loves being known as our Savior! Notice once again the personal call to us:

> Come unto *me*, all ye that labour and are heavy laden, and I will give you rest. Take my yoke upon you, and learn of *me*; for I am meek and lowly in heart: and ye shall find rest unto your souls. For my yoke is [tailor-made], and my burden is light (Matthew 11:28–30, emphasis mine).

We need to draw a couple of conclusions from this passage. First, any attempt to solve life's problems apart from the knowledge of and relationship with Jesus Christ will result in failure. Apart from Him we will not find rest for our souls. He is clear that we cannot live lives filled with temporal matters while ignoring eternal matters. We must turn to Him.

Secondly, anything we turn to apart from Him in order to make life work is another "savior"—a competing god. When we go through challenging times, we dare not merely distract our minds with entertainment or lean on other people for our solutions.

Matthew 11:28–30 is an invitation of a loving Master to be a continued Savior to His people. He wants us to come to Him so that He can show His strength in our weakness. I hope you have seen through this study the disposition of our wonderful God to you. He wants to be your loving, merciful, wise, and powerful Savior!

MAINTAINING A QUIET SOUL REQUIRES SATURATION—THE DISCIPLINE OF MEDITATION[1]

The apostle James instructs us about the necessity and the components of meditating on the Word of God.

> Wherefore lay apart all filthiness and [rampant wickedness], and receive with meekness the engrafted word, which is able to save your souls. But be ye doers of the word, and not hearers only, deceiving your own selves. For if any be a hearer of the word, and not a doer, he is like unto a man beholding his natural face in a [mirror]: for he beholdeth himself, and goeth his way, and [immediately] forgetteth what manner of man he was. But whoso looketh into the perfect law of liberty, and continueth therein, he being not a forgetful hearer, but a doer of the work, this man shall be blessed in his deed. (James 1:21–25)

This passage teaches, first of all, that meditation requires *concentration*. James says "whoso *looketh* into the perfect law of liberty." There is a certain activity we are to be involved in. The word *looketh* is the Greek word *parakupto*. It means to lean over and peer intently into. It is what someone does when he has lost his contact in the carpet. He gets down on all fours, keeps everyone away from the area, and scours the carpet as best he can with his good eye to find the contact. He is "peering intently into." This describes the diligent search and intensity that meditation involves.

Meditation is not the quick overview of a "drive-by devotional." It is the purposeful, intentional search for the knowledge of God and His ways when we open our Bible and read it. We read with the purpose of hearing something from God so that we can do it (Joshua 1:8). The "best end" of our walk with God is to become a Christlike "doer of the work" (James 1:25). The "best means" for that is this purposeful search for an understanding of God and His ways.

The object of that search is the Word of God. It is the only place we can find the truth about God and about how His world works. When our lives are full of noise, we have been living in a fantasy world made up of our own imaginations about what God is like and our own conclusions about how His world works. We believe a lie, and as we have seen, the disintegration of that way of thinking is predictable. The goal of that search is a changed lifestyle—for us to be a "doer of the work."

Meditation also requires *continuation*. James says, "whoso looketh . . . and continueth therein" (1:25). We might ask ourselves, "How long do we continue looking into this passage we are studying?" I asked myself this question the first time I seriously meditated upon James 1:25. I had looked up what *parakupto* meant. I had seen that I was to peer intently into the Word of God, but I didn't have any idea yet how long to "continue" doing that. I prayed and asked God to show me what He meant.

Part of the answer to that prayer came in the next phrase: "He being not a forgetful hearer." I was to continue in the passage meditating upon its truths and its applications for my life until what I was learning took on a measure of permanence—until I can't forget it. Sometimes that takes going back to the passage daily for several weeks.

Most of us know exactly what I'm talking about. We have been reading the Scriptures and pondering a portion of it knowing that there is something in the passage that God really wants us to know. After we have given it considerable thought, God begins to open our eyes and we see the truth with illuminated understanding. When that happens, we rarely forget the truth. We have seen the truth of it from God Himself, and the imprint upon our soul is powerful! Every time we come across that passage our heart warms as we remember the work of God in our soul as we meditated upon His Word. God intends for His truth to have profound effect upon our minds and hearts, but that will come only with intentional meditation.

There was yet another part of the answer to my question, "How long do we continue looking into this passage?" The second part is until we are a "doer of the work"—we are productive. Paul captures this in 1 Timothy 4:15–16.

> Meditate upon these things; give thyself wholly to them; that thy profiting may appear to all. Take heed unto thyself, and unto the [teaching]; continue in them: for in doing this thou shalt both [spare] thyself, and them that hear thee.

Meditation should result in obvious spiritual impact that others can see. The process not only will profit us—as it transforms our lives—but it will profit others who will be convicted, encouraged, and instructed by our lives as they are changed by the process of meditation on the Word.

MAINTAINING A QUIET SOUL REQUIRES STRUCTURE

Our culture scorns structure. This is one of the reasons it is falling apart. In contrast, Paul says,

> Discipline yourself for the purpose of godliness; for bodily discipline is only of little profit, but godliness is profitable for all things, since it holds promise for the present life and also for the life to come (1 Timothy 4:7b–8 NASB).

Godliness is intentional, not accidental. Software applications today come preprogrammed to default to certain settings. If you want the settings to come up differently, you have to override the default. Our human hearts do not come programmed by default for godliness. If we want to be godly, we must intentionally do something different from our natural "settings." We don't stumble into godliness. While God's Spirit is the One Who ultimately changes us, we must do some things that will promote that change.

Paul's choice of words here is interesting. The Greek word translated "discipline" here is *gumnazo*. It is the word from which we get the word *gymnasium*. The word suggests training and exertion. If we are going to "get in shape" spiritually, we must come to the gym and practice until we profit from the effort.

When I turned forty, I began to experience splitting headaches by the end of the day in the office. My colleague and friend Ted Harris, who is now with the Lord, was my family doctor. I asked Ted one day why I was experiencing the headaches. He told me that they were caused by muscular tension in my upper shoulders and neck because of the way I sat at my desk all day leaning over reading paperwork, typing on my keyboard, or counseling students. The problem was postural.

He asked me what kind of exercise I was getting. I told him, "My dictation thumb gets a real workout." He replied, "You're telling me you really don't get any exercise, aren't you?" I admitted that was true. He invited me to join him and several other men who played racquetball at BJU's fitness center every Monday, Wednesday, and Friday at 6 a.m. He said that I would experience some immediate effect on the headaches from the upper body workout I would get from the sport and advised me about how I could improve my posture at the desk as well.

I protested that I was so out of shape I would probably have a heart attack. He said, "That's OK; I'm a doctor. You need to join us." To profit from the sport I had to learn some new disciplines. I had to schedule to be there at 5:45 those three days of the week. I had to learn about stretching and warming up. I had to learn about serving, scoring, forehand and backhand returns, and care of my racquet and glove, and so forth.

Dr. Harris was telling me, "Train yourself in racquetball for the purpose of fitness." It would not happen accidentally; it required intentional structure and discipline. If we are to "get in shape" spiritually, we must also train ourselves. We must learn and practice some new disciplines and structure our lives to make those disciplines a part of our daily routine.

Reading the Word is warming up and stretching. Without much effort at all most adults can read through the Bible at least once a year. That is hardly deep Bible study or even meditation. It is just the beginning. It is merely a warm up; it stretches our muscles of concentration and comprehension. Studying the Word and meditating upon the Word are the real exercise.

Like physical exercise, you may be able to do only small blocks of Bible reading and studying when you first begin. Daily sitting still while reading and thinking about what you read may be very awkward at first— just as trying to chase a racquetball around the court was extremely awkward for me at the start. The following simple hints should get you started if you are new to this discipline.[2]

Establish a regular time. Many Christians find that early morning is best since their first thoughts can be of spiritual things (Psalm 5:3).

Get alone. Shut yourself up in a room away from the distractions of people and technology if possible (Matthew 6:6).

Have a pen and notebook ready. Proverbs 10:14 says, "Wise men [store] up knowledge." Write down anything that God points out to you from His Word.

Include the following elements in your quiet time.

- Bible Reading—Before you begin, ask God to show you something just for you (Psalm 119:18). Follow a Bible-reading schedule so that your reading is not haphazard. Some believers find that including the chapter of Proverbs that corresponds to the day of the month is helpful. Read until God points out something especially for you. Jot down the verse and your immediate thoughts about it. As you read, God will convict you of sin. Write down your decision to forsake these sins, confess them to God, and ask for power to overcome them in your prayer time. God uses His Word to cleanse us (John 15:3). Thank Him for what He has shown you in your reading and share these special verses and insights with others (1 John 1:3).

- Meditation—Use the MAP Method found in appendix C for one way to help you concentrate on God's Word to learn its truths.

- Prayer—Keep a personal prayer journal, using the PRAY acronym:

    Praise: What have you seen today from God that quiets your soul?

    Repent: What has God shown you this week that needs to be confessed to Him and forsaken?

    Ask: What burdens and concerns should you bring to God rather than worrying about them?

Yield: Where do you need to humble yourself before God and give up something you are stubbornly holding on to?

We tend to forget the times of praise. Without them, however, our prayer life becomes a shallow "give me" time. Your times of praise will become easier as you see God answer your requests. Every prayer won't include all four elements, but none of them should be missing from your regular prayer life.

If you have a hard time getting started, consult with your pastor or another mature Christian who spends daily time with God. That person will be more than willing to help you and encourage you in your daily pursuit of Christlikeness through the study of God's Word and fellowship with God about what He has shown you in the Scriptures.

In addition to these daily times in the Word fellowshiping with God, your growth will be further enhanced as you fellowship with God's people during your faithful attendance at a Bible-preaching church. There you will hear God's Word preached by the shepherd God has appointed for that local flock, and you will benefit from the spiritual encouragement and admonishment of other believers in the body of Christ.

These spiritual disciplines should become part of your routine in life. Routine is crucial to anything productive—physically or spiritually. Most people with noisy souls have not established much productive routine in their lives. Routine can help you in the following ways.

Have a morning routine. Get up at a prescribed time, meet with the Lord in private devotions to read the Word, pray, and meditate upon what you have learned. Listen to audio files of sermons while you exercise, get ready in the morning, or drive to and from work (see www.SermonAudio.com). These provide another opportunity for you to saturate your mind with God's ways.

Have an evening routine. Get to bed early enough to be refreshed when you meet the Lord in the morning (determine your bedtime by your morning requirement).

Have a weekend routine. Avoid all activities that will undo everything you have been working on during the week in your spiritual life. Don't vegetate on the couch watching hours of movies or ballgames all weekend—especially if you haven't spent significant time with God during the week. This is a wonderful "catch-up" time to read and study the Scriptures and good Christian books or Bible studies.

Consider devoting a Saturday to "Spending a Day with God" on a quarterly basis. Look at appendix D for instructions on this special time to build your walk with God.

Each weekend make sure you are in a Bible-preaching church on the Lord's Day (Sunday) as mentioned above.

Have a ministry routine. Be about your Father's business. Find a regular opportunity of ministry through your local church. There are usually opportunities for helping with the youth group, nursing home services, children's church services, the bus ministry, a children's Bible club, Sunday school, and church visitation.

Don't overlook the ministry opportunities each day at work or when shopping. Carry gospel tracks in your purse or pocket and look for opportunities to share the good news that Jesus died for sinners with those you meet.

Have a check-up routine. Read Christian books and attend annual Christian marriage conferences if you are married, missions conferences, evangelistic services, Christian life seminars, and Christian men's or ladies' retreats. It is easy for your spiritual and marital life to drift unless you benchmark your Christian life and marriage experiences against the principles of God's Word.

Don't ever scorn routine! It is the flywheel—the conserving power— behind anything productive. Sometimes people today look down their noses at routines and tradition because either can easily become mindless. That certainly is true, but the solution isn't to abandon good habits and practices. The solution is to engage your thinking in the activity.

God ordained daily sacrifices and annual feasts for the instruction and spiritual improvement of the children of Israel. Human nature being what it is, it did not take long for them to continue with the externals but with hearts that were far from God. God didn't abolish the sacrifices and the feasts; He called His people to thoughtful participation. The remedy for us is the same today for any spiritual discipline that helps us maintain an effective walk with God.

MAINTAINING A QUIET SOUL
REQUIRES SUBORDINATION

All of life must be brought under the Lordship of Jesus Christ as we learn what His will is for us in His Word. There is no spiritual growth without bowing before Jesus Christ in humble submission to His desires. We are to study His Word in order to fellowship with Him and to do what He says. God told Joshua,

> This Book of the Law shall not depart from your mouth, but you shall meditate on it day and night, so that you may be careful to do according to all that is written in it (Joshua 1:8 ESV).

Our stability lies in our obedience to what God says. We dare not allow ourselves to be mere "hearers of the Word." We must become "doers" (James 1:21–25). Because God has made such amazing provisions for our life as believers through His grace and because He has given His Word for our understanding, we must take His Word seriously and obey what He says.

With this kind of Savior, the saturation of His Word in our minds in structured study and meditation, and hearts that will subordinate themselves to His will, we can have by God's grace quiet souls.

Take Time to Reflect

1. You learned in this chapter that "maintaining a quiet soul requires a Savior." What have you learned about your Savior, Jesus Christ, through this study? How have your views about Him changed? What has He showed you about Himself that has made an impact upon you? Summarize your thoughts.

2. Set some goals for the days ahead. What degree of regularity and structure would you like to see in your life in the following areas?

Reading the Word

Studying the Word

Memorizing the Word

Hearing the Word in a Bible-preaching church

Witnessing

Praying

Epilogue

WHERE DO YOU GO FROM HERE?

Those who find the material in this book especially helpful should consider going through *Quieting a Noisy Soul*, an interactive, multimedia personal counseling program, since it offers a much more robust application of the truths contained in these pages plus thirteen additional topics not covered in this book. It is made up of four *Quieting a Noisy Soul* seminar DVDs with twenty-four half-hour video sessions, an mp3 CD of all twenty-four seminar sessions, a syllabus and study guide, and a meditation/relaxation CD of Scripture reading, music, and relaxation exercises.

Many have used the program to overcome the grips of destructive eating patterns of anorexia nervosa and bulimia nervosa, obsessive thoughts and compulsive behaviors, panic attacks and other anxiety issues, depression, guilt, and anger. Its strength is the *structured study* and the *saturation* of biblical truth built into the twenty-four weekly study guide sessions. In addition, the study guide contains over one hundred pages of appendix articles, which supplement the video lectures.

While not everyone needs the thoroughness of the interactive personal counseling program to overcome immediate issues in his or her own life, anyone can profit immensely from going through the entire interactive program—especially if he or she ministers to others, including his or her own children. A person will become very aware as he goes through the study that the Scriptures do, indeed, provide "all things that pertain unto [eternal] life and godliness [in this life]" (2 Peter 1:3). Additional counseling helps and a full description of the complete counseling program are available at www.QuietingANoisySoul.com. Small groups will find the *Quieting a Noisy Soul Leader's Guide* especially helpful. It is also a free download from the website.

Your stability and usefulness to God is dependent upon your knowledge of and trust in Who God is and how He works. You must know what is true about God and order your life accordingly. As I said earlier, most believers—even those who have been saved for some time—do not know God well. Consequently, they have noisy souls.

If you are facing serious issues in your life, however, just reading this book will probably not be enough for you to see lasting change. I would recommend that you turn your attention to the full *Quieting a Noisy Soul Counseling Program* and use this book as a review of the truths you learn after you have been through the program. Visit www.QuietingANoisySoul.com for more details about the program and check out the "QuickStart" tab for immediate assistance about your particular struggles.

May God bless you with a quiet soul!

For additional resources from Jim Berg and BJU Press, visit the following websites.

- *Changed Into His Image* (www.ChangedIntoHisImage.com)

- *Created for His Glory* (www.CreatedForHisGlory.com)

- *When Trouble Comes* (www.WhenTroubleComes.com)

- *Quieting a Noisy Soul Counseling Program* (www.QuietingANoisySoul.com)

- *Essential Virtues* (www.EssentialVirtues.com)

- *God Is More than Enough* (www.GodIsMoreThanEnough.com)

See also the author's personal website: www.JimBerg.com for additional resources for Christian growth.

Appendices

Appendix A

HOW TO BECOME A CHRISTIAN

Let me ask you a personal question. "If you were to die today from a terminal illness or in some tragic accident and you were to stand before God, how would you answer God when He asked you this question: 'Why should I let you into My heaven?'"[1]

Some people feel that because they have been deeply religious and have obeyed the Ten Commandments[2] most of the time, God should let them into heaven. Others feel that because they have lived by the Golden Rule[3] and have been honest and moral in their dealings with others, they should be allowed to enter. They say essentially that God should allow them to enter heaven because they have been good in some way.

Jesus predicted that many people would come to Him on that day and would say exactly those things. He says that His reply to them will be "I never knew you: depart from me, ye that [practice sin]" (Matthew 7:23). You see, no matter how many good things we have done, the factor that will keep us out of heaven is our sin.

The Bible makes it clear that "all have sinned, and come short of the glory of God" (Romans 3:23). That means that all of us have lived as if we are important and God doesn't matter. We instinctively place ourselves first instead of God and turn to our "own way" (Isaiah 53:6).

Even our effort to get to heaven by being good shows our rebellion against God because He said that there is no way any of us can be good enough to merit heaven. Every one of us has broken His commandments—and has done so many times. He very clearly said that the "wages of sin is [eternal] death" (Romans 6:23). That means that all of us, because of our rebellion of going our own stubborn way in life, deserve the everlasting punishment of hell because of our mutiny against the Creator.

137

GOOD NEWS!

The good news for us is that eternal life—life in heaven with Jesus Christ forever—is not something we have to earn. It is a gift! Though "the wages of sin is [eternal] death; . . . the gift of God is eternal life through Jesus Christ our Lord" (Romans 6:23). That is good news because the Bible also tells us that it is "not by works of righteousness which we have done, but according to his mercy he saved us" (Titus 3:5). God is willing to mercifully give us a gift we cannot earn. He wants to give us eternal life. But that gift must be personally received by us.

The student center on the campus of Bob Jones University operates a lost and found area for the students. If the lost item has a name on it, the staff notifies the student to come pick it up. If there is no name on it, the staff holds it for several weeks and then disposes of it or sells it for a small price at a lost and found sale. The staff is willing to let the student have his property, but he must come by and show his identification card to claim it.

Salvation from the eternal punishment of our sins is available to everyone, but we, too, must personally claim it.

How can salvation be a free gift? Though it is free to us, it cost Jesus Christ everything. You see, our sins against God require that a penalty be paid. Sinning against our Creator is such a great offense that the only just penalty is eternal suffering and separation from God Himself in hell. Hell is the result of God's granting man his request—"God, leave me alone." We may not realize it, but that is essentially what we say to God every time we reject His way and live life our own way. That is the bad news for the sinner.[4]

The good news is that God loves us and arranged for His own Son to live on this earth to pay the penalty for us. Though Jesus lived in a body like ours, He did not share our sinful and stubborn nature. He lived a sinless life in complete obedience to His Father while on the earth. He qualified—as a perfect sacrificial lamb—to die in our place. Look at these chilling but wonderful words from the Old Testament, which predicted the sacrificial death of Jesus Christ on the cross for us.

> He was wounded for *our* transgressions, he was bruised for *our* iniquities: the chastisement [for] *our* peace was upon him; and

with his stripes *we* are healed. All we like sheep have gone astray; we have turned every one to his own way; and the Lord hath laid on him the iniquity of us all (Isaiah 53:5–6, emphasis mine).

The apostle John states the same thing this way:

For God so loved the world, that he gave his only begotten Son, that whosoever believeth in him should not perish, but have everlasting life. . . . He that believeth on him is not condemned: but he that believeth not is condemned already, because he hath not believed in the name of the only begotten Son of God (John 3:16, 18).

Jesus' sacrifice of His own blood as the eternal payment for anyone who would believe on Him satisfied the righteous anger of God against our mutiny. All that is left is for us to admit to God that we are indeed hell-deserving sinners, realize that Jesus died in our place and arose from the dead, and then accept the gift of eternal life from God. It is a simple plan—one that even a child can understand. A child will cry out for help to the person he believes will help him. A sinner who wants the gift of eternal life can come to Jesus Christ by praying a prayer like this.

Lord Jesus, I realize that I am a sinner. I have not obeyed You. I have gone my own way many times. Since You are perfect and Your heaven is perfect, I realize that even one sin disqualifies me from heaven.[5] I repent of my sin and ask Your forgiveness. I accept Your gift of eternal life. I want Your substitutionary death to be applied to my sin account.[6] Cleanse me from my sin and make me one of Your own children.[7] Thank You for loving me and for saving me.

Share your decision with a Bible-preaching pastor or mature Christian friend who will want to help you grow in your newfound spiritual life.[8]

Appendix B

THE STORIES OF JENNIE AND ANNE

I have heard from many people like Jennie and Anne over the past several years. God has transformed these believers who struggled with the challenges of panic attacks, eating disorders, psychosis, bipolar behaviors, obsessive thoughts and compulsive behaviors, and many other manifestations of noisy souls.

I would warn you, however, that their transformations did not come without much time in the Word and much humility and transparency before God and others. Jesus said that if we try to save our life, we will lose it, but if we lose our life for His sake, we will find it (Matthew 16:24–25). In both of these cases God used a godly pastor and an understanding and supportive husband to help them through the rough times. I trust you will gain much hope as you see another testimony of how a believer has been "transformed by the renewing of [her] mind" (Romans 12:2).

From Jennie

"Here is my testimony of how God used *Quieting a Noisy Soul* to go from seventeen years on antidepressants to being completely drug free. If there is even one person who will be prevented from starting psychiatric medications or encouraged to stop them, all my years of suffering will have been worth it.

"I was unsaved and using drugs and alcohol to fill the hole in my heart where the Lord wanted to live. I started on antidepressants in 1990. On December 19, 1996 I realized I was a sinner, confessed every sin I could think of, and asked the Lord Jesus Christ to save me, help me live for Him, and take control of my life.

"My husband and I embraced our life in Christ and I thought my problems were over. I never thought to stop the medications because the doctors told me I would need them for the rest of my life. That was reinforced every time I tried to quit on my own, and the depression would come tumbling back worse than it had been previously. I was a registered nurse and trusted my doctors.

"Shortly after being saved I became pregnant with our daughter and had to stop the antidepressants. I was a brand new Christian so I did not know what to do when my depression returned along with the withdrawal symptoms. Throughout the pregnancy I struggled with the depression and started back on the drugs after my daughter was born. I had no idea that I was addicted.

"I was on antidepressants for fifteen years before I saw what they were doing to me. I cannot tell you how many doctors and well-meaning friends used the analogy, 'If a diabetic needed insulin you would not think it was a sin to take insulin.' I see now that was comparing apples with oranges. A diabetic is deficient in insulin; a depressed person is not deficient in Prozac!

"Antidepressants no more cure depression than a pain pill heals a broken leg. You could NEVER have convinced me a few years ago that I did not have a chemical imbalance that I had no control over. We tried moving, changing churches, having another baby, and yet nothing stopped the sense of hopelessness.

"On the outside my life was great. I had a wonderful husband, a terrific church, and was homeschooling two beautiful children—and yet, I was miserable. I could not stop the thoughts that my children and husband would be so much better off without me. As a Christian I knew I could not take my own life, but how I pleaded with the Lord to let me die.

"Every day I would wake up thinking, 'How am I going to make it through this day?' Every night I would promise myself that tomorrow would be better. However, each day was worse than the day before. The pain in my heart was so intense it was unbearable. I understood why people hurt themselves. It seemed like real physical pain would hurt so much less than the psychological torture I put myself through day after day.

"The self-loathing knew no bounds. I had a long list of causes of my depression—from my mother-in-law to multiple miscarriages to my failing health. The doctors told me repeatedly that a chemical imbalance was the cause of my chronic major depression. I lived in fear that my children would inherit this chemical imbalance and dread each day as I did.

"My doctors put me on every antidepressant on the market, one after another. Each time my dose would get raised to the maximum level and eventually quit working, so they would try another. Finally, my doctors decided that one medication alone would not be enough for my severe case, so they decided I needed to try two together. The result was unrelenting migraines. I added medication for the migraines to the antidepressants. The extreme exhaustion from the medications and chronic fatigue led them to medicate me to wake me up. I had not slept well in years so they decided that a lack of sleep was my problem. They added medication to help me sleep.

"I started having anxiety attacks so they gave me drugs for that. Not surprisingly, my brain was all befuddled, and I could not concentrate so my doctors decided I had adult ADD and put me on medication for that.

"I kept trying to tell them that something was not right after the last medication change. I started acting in ways I had never known before. My husband was concerned about our children, and to my horror he would not allow me to homeschool any longer and put the children in a Christian school. I had failed in the most important job in my life! I had failed my children, my husband, and the Lord.

"Suddenly I had a new excuse for all my problems. I was left alone with all my problems. I spent all day soaking in my misery, and I sunk deeper and deeper into depression. I believed all the lies that my self-centered heart could generate: 'You are a failure; you are crazy; your family would be better off without you; you can't do anything right; you have no purpose; no one needs or wants you.'

"Three months later I ended up in my worst nightmare. I ended up locked up in a psychiatric ward. My husband thought he was putting me there to help me. The psychiatrist told me, 'Psychiatry is about two things—drugs and talking, and I'm not here to talk.' By the time I was discharged two weeks later I was on ten different medications. I could no longer read or write because I could not concentrate. I could not remember anything that happened from one minute to the next. In the following weeks I asked my doctor repeatedly if I had suffered a stroke or a seizure because I felt like parts of my brain were gone.

"My children were suffering a great deal because of my dysfunction. God gave amazing grace to my husband during this time. My dear pastor told me, 'I don't know how to help you, but I'm going to try.'

He and his wife came to my house week after week ministering to me with devotionals on the joy of the Lord. I had never felt so loved, and yet I felt like even more of a failure because I did not have any joy. I could not concentrate enough to read my Bible and seriously doubted my salvation.

"Then one day my pastor gave my husband the *Quieting a Noisy Soul Counseling Program*. I received it gladly because I couldn't read and this was something I could watch and listen to. From the first lesson I knew my life was going to change. I had hope!

"The lectures described me exactly. It was a gift from the Lord. I listened to the messages over and over and over. I listened to the mp3 audio files as I worked in my home, as I ferried the children to and from school, as I shopped, and during the countless hours that I lay awake at night unable to sleep.

"I prayed as David prayed in Psalm 139 that the Lord would search me and try me. Amazingly, I was able to memorize Isaiah 41:10, and I clung to it like a life preserver in a sea of despair.

"After a few weeks of listening, a light went on. I realized the medications were keeping my brain from understanding and enjoying a relationship with God. That day I decided I would go off those medications. I knew my pastor, my husband, and certainly my doctors would not want me to take such a serious step, but I felt like I needed to do it.

"So, armed with my STOP-THINK cards, my mp3 player, and my Bible (on mp3), I began. The withdrawals were scary to say the least! It became very clear to my husband and me that I was addicted to the medications.

"I spent the next two years listening to the sessions nearly 24/7 as I completely weaned myself off every one of those ten drugs. Every day I was growing stronger physically and spiritually. I began the painful process of reconciling with people I had wronged. I started to experience peace and joy for the first time in years. [See note of caution on regarding drug withdrawal on pages 146–47 at this end of this testimony.]

"I would stumble and resist humbling myself, but the encouraging words of the sessions would remind me not to give up. There were times when I wanted to go back to the security of the drugs.

"I had to learn to deal with feelings I had not experienced for fifteen years. I had episodes of rage that scared even me. I thought maybe I really am mentally ill. Then I would remember the words of the sessions: 'The Lord gives you more than you think you can handle because He wants you to trust Him. Your problem is spiritual; there is a cure, and His name is Jesus.' So I would carry on.

"I can happily report that I have been off drugs for eighteen months now. I am still suffering from the effects of brain-damaging medications, however. I have a long way to go, but I spent seventeen years putting medication between my soul and a real relationship with Christ, so I feel like a babe in Christ.

"After three and a half years I am still learning from those same twenty-four lessons. They led me to the cross with my pain, and there I laid my burden down. Hopelessness is a spiritual problem, no matter how it starts, but I am here to say that because Christ used *Quieting a Noisy Soul*, it can end. If I can learn to function without medications and can experience joy and peace, then anyone can.

"My struggles are not over. I may always have to fight those defeated thoughts. The difference is that now I have the tools to know how to use the Word of God to carry me through. I know how to 'preach myself a sermon' as the sessions taught me, instead of listening to the lies of my heart.

"I want to conclude my testimony with an overview of the truths God taught me over the past three and a half years. These truths stabilized my soul.

"The root of my problem was unbelief. I had to learn how to dig, dig, dig for truth. I had to stop listening to myself and start listening to God. It did not come easy for me.

"I was the person you talked about who said, 'God loves everyone, but He does not love me.' He showed me right out of the gate that I was not believing Him. He reminds us repeatedly in the Word that He loves us and wants us to have peace. He forced me to admit to myself that if I could not believe that He loved me then how could I say that I believed the Bible at all?

"Once I was able to start accepting that, He started showing me ways that He loved me that had been there all along, but I had failed to recognize them. The rest came much easier.

"Next, the Lord taught me that because He loves me I could trust Him completely no matter what happened. I looked up every verse I could find about trust and how the Lord would take care of me and never leave me, and I meditated upon them. When I was in pain and crying I would pray for help to resist the urge to dwell on my misery. He would bring verses to mind that reminded me that 'He was always up to something good in my life,' and I did not have to see the good to know it was there.

"Then He taught me that peace comes from the knowledge of God. I thought I knew God, but I learned that you can't just 'know' God and move on. To really know God you have to have a close, personal, ongoing relationship with Him. I had to study His Word, pray, and obey!

"If I was going to show God that I loved Him I needed to obey no matter what. That included the painful process of removing sin from my life. I quickly realized that using drugs to do for me what He wanted to do, for me was sin. My pet sin was dwelling on my misery and ruminating about what other people thought of me. I needed to shift my focus from myself and other people to the only One that really matters—my God.

"The Lord allowed me to be completely bedridden in order to focus entirely on Him. He showed me that I could obey Him even if I was not able to get out of bed. Through panic attacks the Lord taught me that He had not given me the spirit of fear. I learned to 'track my thoughts, not my feelings.'

"I used the STOP-THINK cards to remind myself that 'God is always good—always!' and 'God is always great—always!' He showed me that I am never alone, and that He is always in control, and that no matter what, He never changes!

"Finally, the Lord showed me that this work is not going to end. Sanctification is an ongoing process that will require effort on my part every day of my life if I am going to stay at peace. I can tell you that no amount of effort is too high a price to pay for a quiet soul!

"I know now that it is okay to hurt, to suffer, and to fail, and that I cannot lose my salvation. I know that if I abide in Christ, His peace is always available. Hopelessness will remain a thing of the past if I keep my eyes focused on the Lord. I have hope because a loving God is in control of my life.

"If someone would tell me I would suffer for three years of drug withdrawal symptoms, I would have said, 'Forget the whole thing!' Within a week of realizing I was no longer having withdrawal symptoms I thought, 'That wasn't so bad. I would have gone through ten times that to be free from those drugs.' My husband and I are reminded continually just how blessed we are that I am no longer in bondage.

"Thank you is not enough. How can I thank you for pointing me to the only true healing? How can I thank you for creating audio and video files so that I was never alone with my wicked thoughts, and for speaking comforting words into my ear as I drove that painful route to take my children to school each day when I knew that was not what the Lord originally wanted? There are not enough words to thank you for pointing me to God who gave my children and my husband their mother and wife back.

"We returned to homeschooling last year and we just started our second year back. I can remember things now; I can read; I can write; I have reignited friendships that I had ignored for years; I have started new friendships. I talk to my family across the continent on a regular basis now.

"I can feel pain for the first time in years—and I know what to do about it! I pray; I thank the Lord, and I meditate on Who He is and keep going. I know that the Lord will uphold me with the right hand of His righteousness. I can sleep—because my soul is quiet."

Cautions Regarding Drug Withdrawal

Because of the serious side effects of withdrawal and of having to face all the problems of living that the medications mask, it is not advisable to attempt medication withdrawals without the cooperation and oversight of a physician and the support and understanding of family members close by. Jennie's nursing experience and the support of those around her were crucial to the success of her withdrawal.

If you are on psychiatric medication and are contemplating coming off them, consult your physician. If neither he nor you are aware of what is involved with withdrawal, consult *Your Drug May Be Your Problem* by Peter R. Breggin, MD, and David Cohen, PhD (Cambridge, MA: Perseus Publishing, 1999). Breggin, a secular psychiatrist, is spearheading a movement within the American Psychiatric Association to return to "talk therapy" and to abandon drug treatments for all psychiatric disorders. His clinic and many associated with it are treating every psychiatric condition, including psychosis, successfully without drugs (as successful as the world can accomplish without God). The secular literature against psychiatric drugs is increasing every day. See also www. GenerationRxFilm.com.

When encountering doctors who prescribe psychiatric drugs or people taking such drugs, it is important not to have a critical spirit toward them. If they knew a better way to handle the issues they are attempting to address with drugs, most of them would choose that better way.

For a Christian viewpoint read *Will Medicine Stop the Pain? Finding God's Healing for Depression, Anxiety, and Other Troubling Emotions* by Elyse Fitzpatrick and Laura Hendrickson, MD. Hendrickson is a biblical counselor who formerly practiced psychiatry.

In *Taking Time to Quiet Your Soul* I include extended footnotes on medications for anxiety and depression. Understand the risks and efforts involved before attempting to come off any drugs.

From Anne

"Since I was a little girl, I have struggled with anxiety. I became a Christian at a young age, but my relationship with God always felt distant. I was not growing spiritually, and worry, fear, and despair were my frequent companions. My mother took me to the hospital when I was eight years old because I had been experiencing many episodes of intense pain in my stomach that often left me unable to move. After conducting tests, the doctor finally concluded that the pain was stress induced. But my doctor, teacher, and parents could not figure out what was causing me to have such anxious thoughts.

"As a teenager, I started feeling angry as well as anxious, and I experienced many periods of depression. I would sometimes sit in my closet wailing and desperately crying out to God for help. When the pain did not disappear, I felt abandoned and unloved by God. I sought help in the church but left feeling extremely discouraged and alone. My relationship with my parents was deteriorating as well. When I was fifteen, I took some pills and left the bottle out for my parents to find. I desperately wanted and needed help.

"I started to see a psychiatrist and Christian psychologist, and things got worse as I was constantly put on one new medication after another and given first one and then a new diagnosis and then another. I had so many negative side effects from these drugs, and my depression and anxiety only worsened.

"When I was sixteen years old, I was unable to cope with the pressures in my life, and I stopped going to church and finally was unable to continue in school, so was forced to complete my high school classes in a homebound program. I had been a straight A student, but now I barely had the emotional energy to meet the teachers who came to my house. As I continually struggled with thoughts of suicide, I pleaded with my parents to find a place or person that could help me. My parents learned of a hospital in another state that provided Christian counseling. My parents were willing to do anything to help me, and they found the money to put me into the hospital. It was not at all what I had hoped for, and I couldn't wait to leave after two weeks.

"A few months after coming home, I starting doing something that I never thought I would do in order to cope with the pain that I was feeling inside. I started to cut myself. The physical pain of these cuts was the only thing that would numb my mental agony. Then when I was seventeen, I was so desperate to end my misery that I deliberately overdosed on one of my meds. It is amazing that I lived after losing consciousness, but God had other plans for me.

"I continued to struggle for several years with depression, eating disorders, and anxiety attacks, and I was unable to stay in college or keep a job for more than a few short weeks or months at a time. I even went long periods without seeing other family members or friends. I missed many holiday events with my extended family. I felt as though I was just rotting and wasting away in my parent's house. For years, my parents had been praying for me and asking God for help, but I still felt that there was a barrier between God and me.

"In my early twenties I had a few years during which I was able to function better, but I still felt as though God was far away from me and couldn't hear me. I started dating Martin, one of my brother's best friends whom I had known since I was thirteen years old. He knew of my struggles, and he was patient, kind, and supportive.

"Not many months after we were married, I started to struggle again, and Martin often felt helpless to counsel me or to provide solutions. On my own I decided to go off my medications (after 10 years of being on many different ones), and the withdrawal symptoms were very difficult. I had times where I experienced intense rage, and I often felt that I might lose control. After a short time of doing better, I became pregnant. My husband and I had not found a church yet, but we felt a strong desire to find a church home before our son was born. We found a wonderful church and made some important changes in our lives. I still felt uneasy about being a mother and having a little person depend on me while I still struggled to cope with different pressures.

"Immediately after my son was born, I couldn't sleep at all, and I was very anxious. The nurses and my doctor were concerned about my anxiety and insomnia, and things went downhill when we took our little baby home from the hospital. I had only slept three hours in four days, and I was physically and mentally exhausted. The baby would not sleep and cried and cried during the night. I was consumed with worry and fear, and I could not get any relief from the relentless, desperately anxious thoughts. I couldn't handle being around my son, and I felt that I was losing my mind. I felt physically ill, and my thoughts tortured me night and day.

"My dad took me to a hospital, and some wonderful nurses took me under their wings and spoke encouraging words to me. I was given sleeping pills and sent home. The pills barely helped, and I could still sleep for only two or three hours at night. I was sent to a psychiatrist who started me on an antidepressant and anti-anxiety drug. The anti-anxiety medication only knocked me out for a couple of hours, and then the mental torture began as soon as I woke up. My parents had to come help us with our son because I could not take care of him. The anxious thoughts were crippling, and I felt such despair during this time. There were times that I would literally writhe on the floor because nothing would stop those agonizing thoughts, and I could no longer just shut down or turn to cutting to relieve my pain. I felt like a hunted, tortured animal.

"My husband called our pastor and asked him to come to our house. I had great doubts that he would be able to help me, and I almost refused to meet with him. I am so grateful that I did because the message he shared with me changed my life.

Some of the women in our church had been meeting together and watching the series *Quieting a Noisy Soul*, and my pastor sat down in our living room and had us watch session 17—'Overcoming Your Anxiety and Fear, Part 1.'

"[You] described how my emotions were just reacting to my thoughts and that my thoughts and conclusions were affecting my feelings and my body. [You] said, 'Worriers meditate on the uncertainties that could happen rather than the certainties of what God is like and what he promises.' That's exactly what I had been doing my entire life! I wanted to feel safe and secure, and if I felt that God wasn't providing that, then I turned to other ways of coping. It was so destructive, and I robbed myself of the opportunities to rest in God's presence and His truths.

"So often in the past, I let my circumstances and fears drive my life, but I needed to 'cling to the things that are true about God no matter what is happening to you.' I had been told by doctors that I should change my behavior or thoughts to more 'positive' ones, but that never worked and left me feeling so defeated. As [you] said, 'You don't talk yourself into this frame of mind by human logic; you submit yourself into it by affirming divine truth.'

"[You] provided many verses to be committed to memory, and I put those verses around my house. I clung to them as if my life depended on them, and it did! I was the weary and burdened person in Matthew 11:28-30. I had Isaiah 41:10 on my fridge, and I felt so comforted to know that God was carrying me. My pastor came to the house and shared these truths with me. That very night I was able to sleep through the night—something I hadn't done since my son was born! I had never experienced peace like that before, and I was hungry to know God. 2 Peter 1:2–3 talks about how we can experience this peace when we know God. I had such hope! As [you] said, 'We will not despair if we know God well and are content with what He has provided because we have found Him to be more than enough for us.'

"My battle with anxiety and fear was far from over, but I finally had the weapons to fight it. At first, I had to recite the verses every minute of the day just to get through it. I had to take every thought captive and turn them over to God (2 Corinthians 10:5). I was told that this would be a process, but God would grant me victory! After a few weeks, I found that I wasn't constantly tormented by thoughts, and then I had months where I was free.

"One vital piece of information that I learned is that this is something that has to be a part of my life every single day. I cannot take a vacation from meditating on God's truths without experiencing severe and debilitating consequences. When I accept that He is more than enough for me no matter what is happening in my life, that's when I can rest and feel His joy."

The letter below is from Anne's husband, Martin.

"There's little to compare to the helplessness of watching a loved one 'walk through the valley of the shadow of death.' My wife's extended valleys included periods of seclusion from the outside world, self-inflicted physical wounds to temporarily escape her emotional torment, and angry outbursts at those closest to her. She had gone through years of secular psychiatric treatment including prescriptions to a full array of psychotropic medications beginning in her midteen years. None of this stopped the anxiety, frustration, depression, and feelings of inadequacy that plagued her thoughts. The lack of substantive help only heightened the hopelessness of the dark valleys in which she lived.

"After the birth of our oldest son, those same coping mechanisms culminated in a complete functional breakdown, often finding Anne lying prostrate on the floor, tormented with crippling anxiety. Postpartum care for the anxiety-induced insomnia included the highest dose of sleeping pills and tranquilizers which yielded only minimal sleep. Psychiatric care consisted of yet another antidepressant prescription. Nothing seemed to help . . . and Anne slipped ever deeper into the dark swamp of depressive anxiety.

"I would plead with God in prayer to release Anne from the darkness but the days wore on to weeks and I found my own hope in our Savior severely tested.

"One particularly dark Sunday morning, with tears once again freely flowing, I begged God for help from the solitary heights of the mountain behind our house (Psalm 121). When I came home later that day, Anne had resolved that it would be best to leave me and our son and admit herself to a psychiatric hospital. With pain, confusion, and fear I wondered if this was, in fact, God's answer to my prayer.

"I had been talking to our pastor and called once again. He offered to come to the house the next morning to meet with us. With hopeless agreement I set a time all the while wondering what good it would do. Modern secular psychiatry had been unable to do anything in well over a decade to help Anne and now watched helpless as my wife spiraled into the depths of despair. What could a meeting with our pastor do at this point? But I guessed it couldn't hurt . . .

"That Monday morning, I was again asking for God to heal Anne as she was crippled with anxiety. I thought of the father in Mark 9 who pled with Jesus on behalf of his son to 'have compassion on us, and help us.'

"And although I hadn't verbalized it, I knew Jesus' follow-up question of 'If I can?' was just as valid for me as for that boy's father. I was brought to my knees knowing my belief in the sovereignty and character of God had been shattered and I could do nothing but pray the father's cry, 'I do believe; help my unbelief!'

"Our pastor came later that morning and began addressing Anne's anxiety using the STOP-THINK cards [you] talk about in the program, and we watched video session 17 which specifically deals with anxiety. As Scripture was unpacked by *Quieting a Noisy Soul* and applied to Anne's life, the thick veil of anxiety and depression that darkened her thoughts was torn by the power of God's truth.

"The rest of that day we referred to the STOP-THINK cards and utilized other scriptural tools outlined by [you] to remind us to 'cling to the things that are true about God.' Not only was Anne's attitude changed, she was actually able to sleep through the night for the first time since our son was born!

"In the days that followed, the anxiety dwindled as we worked through other sections of *Quieting a Noisy Soul* and applied the biblically focused approach to applying scriptural solutions. God had emphatically answered my prayers for us while giving us a fresh vision for who He is.

"Since then, we've often commented that life has thrown us many 'real' stresses. These circumstances have served to reinforce the effectiveness of the *Quieting a Noisy Soul's* principles both when actively utilized and when we've become lax and then are forced to return to the biblical insights.

"*Quieting a Noisy Soul* offers a biblically focused and effective approach to dealing with the very real and very crippling effects of anxiety and depression as well as offering a renewed hope for facing everyday struggles of life. Thank you so much for pointing us to our Savior!"

Appendix C

THE MAP METHOD OF MEDITATION

Let me introduce you to a simple way to start getting more out of the Scriptures you study from day to day. I call this the MAP method: Memorize, Analyze, Personalize.

Find a portion of Scripture relevant to your problem or find one that deals with a Bible truth you wish to master. Always meditate on Scripture that God's Spirit "highlights" as you are reading His Word.

Memorize the Passage

Memorizing often occurs automatically if the passage is studied intensely enough in the next step. During temptation you must know exactly what God has said word for word. Merely having a general idea about what is right is not enough when dealing with the deceptive nature of your own heart. A man who cannot remember God's exact words is in danger of leaning on his "own understanding" (Proverbs 3:5).

Many people memorize verses by writing the first letter of each word in a verse. For example, Psalm 119:105 says, "Thy word is a lamp unto my feet, and a light unto my path." The first letters are

T w i a l u m f, a a l u m p.

The first letter of each word (include the punctuation just as it appears in the text) gives enough of a prompt so that you can recall the word, but since the whole word is not present, you do not find yourself merely reading the words mindlessly.

Analyze the Passage

Study the passage, asking the Holy Spirit to give you a thorough understanding of its message. You can do an *intensive* study of the passage by listing the major words of the verses and then using an English dictionary to find out the meaning of each word. If possible, look up each word in a Greek or Hebrew dictionary or check the meaning of each word in *Strong's Exhaustive Concordance*. Once you are sure of each word's meaning, put the passage in your own words (i.e., paraphrase it). A more extensive study would involve using a commentary or a good study Bible to help you understand more about who wrote the passage, to whom it was written, and why it was written. Most important, pray that God will illuminate your understanding. Ask Him to teach you what He wants you to know from the Scriptures.

Personalize the Passage

Plan concrete changes in your life that are consistent with your understanding of the passage. Such plans would include schedules, steps, and details. Ask yourself, "When have I failed to obey this truth in the past? When am I likely to meet a temptation again? What should be the godly response the next time I am tempted?" Think through this "game plan" thoroughly and in advance of the next temptation. Use the passage in a personal prayer to God. For example, a person meditating on James 4:1–11 might begin a prayer this way: "Lord, You tell me here in James 4:1 that the conflict I am having with John is the result of my own lusts—my desires to have something my way. I know that isn't pleasing to You. Instead of responding in anger to John, I need Your help and grace, which You promise in James 4:6 where You said that You resist the proud but give grace to the humble. Help me to humble myself and not to insist on my own way. I want to allow You to lift me up in Your time. . . ."

I think you get the picture—God has so wired us that the only way we can keep from disintegration is to continually return to Him in repentance and dependence. Meditation is a key component in that process (I Timothy 4:15–16).

Appendix D

SEEKING GOD

By now you should realize how important it is to have daily interaction with God. Beyond that, you will benefit greatly by spending some extended times with God. God is not playing games of "hide-and-seek" with us so that just as we feel we are about to get close, He runs away and hides again. In fact, He has just the opposite disposition. He wants us to find Him. Notice His heart in Deuteronomy 4:29.

> But if . . . thou shalt seek the Lord thy God, thou shalt find him,
> if thou seek him with all thy heart and with all thy soul.

In this appendix, I want to suggest some ways that will help you as you make seeking God a lifelong discipline.

SPENDING A DAY WITH GOD

At the close of chapter 3, "Understanding the Solution," you heard the testimony of Liz, who realized her life was out of control and she needed to get away to spend time with God. Her marriage was not fulfilling, she had sleep problems, and she was seriously overweight. In addition, her work situation was disintegrating, and she was growing increasingly depressed. I directed her to a short section in *Changed into His Image* entitled "Spending a Day with God" (pages 156–59). The following text has been adapted from that section.

> I'm sure by now you realize that you cannot change any part of your life without a growing relationship with your Creator. . . . Something must be "going on" between you and God for any real progress to be made.

> Everything God allows in our lives is designed by Him to draw us to Himself in humble submission and dependence. You grow only when you are moving toward that end.

Furthermore, you cannot help others come to know God in this way if you are not walking in this kind of fellowship yourself. If you have not seen much progress in your own walk with Christ, let me suggest that you plan to take a day or weekend off and spend it alone with God. Married couples find it necessary to get alone together on a regular basis to improve their relationship with each other and to build their marriage. Sometimes they annually attend a couple's conference, where, in addition to the sessions on marriage topics, they are able to spend some quiet time together reflecting on their marriage and planning ways to make their relationship stronger. Other couples plan a weekend away on their anniversary for the same purpose. The main idea is to remove themselves from the daily distractions so that they can devote their thoughts and attention to each other and their relationship. Plan a similar "retreat" alone with God.

If your responsibilities will not allow you to take an entire weekend away, at least plan for quarterly outings with God. For example, arrange to free up several hours of a Saturday. Pack a lunch and drive to a local or state park or somewhere else where you will not be around many people. Take your Bible, a notebook, your prayer list, a hymnal, and perhaps a devotional book. Spend your time reading lengthy sections of the Scriptures and writing down what you are learning about God or about your own heart condition. Allow God to bring to your mind any matters that need to be reconciled with Him or others. Write down the names of the people you need to see to make reconciliation so that you do not forget to do so once you return home. Confess your sin to God and praise Him for the promises of His forgiveness.

Take some time to sing praises to Him out of your hymnal. (Go ahead and sing out loud if no one is around, even if you can't carry a tune.) If you absolutely cannot sing, read the words out loud slowly and reflectively so that their meaning can sink into your heart. If you play the guitar, take it with you to accompany yourself, but don't get sidetracked by getting caught up in your practice time with your instrument or "performing" for anyone close by who might hear you. If it will become a distraction in any way to your worship of God, leave it at home.

Set aside some time to get "caught up" on your intercessory prayer for family members, coworkers, spiritual leaders in your life, missionaries, and those enduring great affliction at this time because of illness or disaster. Make note of any "errands of mercy" you could do for them when you return home or spend a few minutes writing a letter of encouragement right then.

Choose a Scripture passage of several verses and meditate on it using the MAP Method of Meditation [discussed in appendix C]. Memorize the passage and spend time prayerfully reflecting on its meaning and application for you. Write out what changes you will need to make in your life to carry out what you learned from God's Word. You must take time for God to speak to you. Ask Him to illumine you by His Spirit. Listen to Him and reflect seriously on what He says.

By now I think you get the idea. You cannot know God "on the run" any more than you can know any other person that way. Personal relationships are not built "efficiently." They take enormous amounts of time devoted to interaction with the other person. (This is why we call our time with God "devotions"; it is time "devoted" to Him.) You will find that your "day with God" will have significant effect upon your regular, daily devotional time with Him. When you spend time with Him each day, though it be only thirty or forty minutes, the depth and quality of the interaction with God will be profoundly different. When you sense the shallowness creeping back in, schedule another "day with God."

Notes

Chapter One

1. *An Expository Dictionary of New Testament Words*, s.v. "weary."
2. *Theological Dictionary of the New Testament*. 1964–c1976. vols. 5–9 ed. Gerhard Friedrich. Vol. 10 compiled by Ronald Pitkin. (G. Kittel, G. W. Bromiley & G. Friedrich, Ed.) (electronic ed.) (9:86–87). Grand Rapids, MI: Eerdmans.
3. Proverbs 3:5–8; 4:22; 16:24; 17:22.
4. Jeremiah 2:13; John 15:4–5; 2 Corinthians 3:3; 4:16–18.

Chapter Two

1. You can download a document featuring these statements about God and listing the references from QuietingaNoisySoul.com/downloads/memory-cards.pdf.
2. The meditation CD, which is a part of the multimedia *Quieting a Noisy Soul Counseling Program*, features all these verses read aloud by the author against the background of traditional Christian hymns. It is especially useful to those who wish to meditate on the Scriptures while driving, doing housework, when having trouble falling asleep in the evening because of noise in the soul, or when your mind is so foggy from prescription drugs that you cannot think clearly enough to read the Scriptures for yourself. Your stability and usefulness to God are dependent upon your knowledge of and trust in Who God is and how He works. You must know what is true about God and order your life accordingly. As I said earlier, most believers—even those who have been saved for some time—do not know God well. Consequently, they have noisy souls.

Chapter Five

1. Sessions 17–19 "Overcoming Anxiety and Fear," Parts 1, 2, and 3 of the *Quieting a Noisy Soul Counseling Program* treat anxiety issues in great depth. See also the website www.QuietingANoisySoul.com for additional information about dealing with anorexia and bulimia.
2. Session 20 "Overcoming Anger and Bitterness" of the *Quieting a Noisy Soul Counseling Program* unpacks the major causes of anger—frustration, hurt, and fear and teaches the viewer how to address each one biblically.
3. Once again please note that sessions 21–22 "Overcoming Despair and Discouragement," Parts 1 and 2 of the *Quieting a Noisy Soul Counseling Program* cover this topic in much more depth.

Chapter Six

1. Thomas Watson, *The Art of Divine Contentment* (Morgan, PA: Soli Deo Gloria Publications, 1653), 19.
2. The actual account of this event is found in Acts 16:16–40.
3. Jeremiah Burroughs, *The Rare Jewel of Christian Contentment* (1648; rpr., Carlisle, PA: Banner of Truth Trust, 1964), 19.
4. Watson., 34.
5. Watson, 35.
6. Henry W. Baker, "The King of Love My Shepherd Is" (1868).

CHAPTER SEVEN
1. A. W. Tozer, *The Knowledge of the Holy* (New York: Harper-Collins, 1961), 7–10.

CHAPTER NINE
1. Walter C. Smith, "Immortal, Invisible, God Only Wise" (1876).
2. Cindy Berry, "Almighty, Unchangeable God" (Delaware Water Gap, PA: Shawnee Press, 1996).
3. Thomas O. Chisholm, "Great Is Thy Faithfulness" (Carol Stream, IL: Hope Publishing Co., 1923. Ren. 1951).
4. Joseph M. Scriven, "What a Friend We Have in Jesus" (1855).
5. Isaac Watts, "O God, Our Help in Ages Past" (1719).

CHAPTER TEN
1. A. W. Pink, *Profiting from the Word* (Edinburgh: Banner of Truth Trust, 1974), 46.
2. *An Expository Dictionary of New Testament Words*, s.v. "power."
3. Walter A. Elwell, *Evangelical Dictionary of Theology* (Grand Rapids: Baker Book House, 1984), 458.
4. A. W. Tozer, *The Attributes of God* (Camp Hill, PA: Christian Publications, 1997), 25.
5. Jerry Bridges, *Trusting God* (Colorado Springs: NavPress, 1988), 26.
6. Bridges, 84
7. *An Expository Dictionary of New Testament Words*, s.v. "right."
8. Bridges, 37.
9. Bridges, 38.

CHAPTER ELEVEN
1. Pink, 19.
2. Bridges, 119.
3. Bridges, 127.
4. Elwell, 455.
5. Tozer, 70.

CHAPTER TWELVE
1. Caution: Biblical meditation is not at all like that which is encouraged by Eastern mystic religions or New Age human potential and creativity movements. These teach that one must empty his mind or focus on himself to discover his hidden potential. These are never taught anywhere in the Scriptures and have nothing in common with biblical meditation.
2. Adapted from *Basics for Believers* by Jim Berg (Greenville, SC: BJU Press, 1978), 18–19.

APPENDIX A

1. Jesus Himself speaks of hell as a place of literal torment. He tells the true account of two men who lived and died. One went to heaven; the other to hell. You can read about it in Luke 16:19–31.
2. Exodus 20:3–17.
3. The Golden Rule: "Do unto others as you would have them do unto you" is a paraphrase of Jesus' statement in Matthew 7:12.
4. Luke 16:19–31.
5. James 2:10.
6. 2 Corinthians 5:21.
7. John 1:12.
8. For your own immediate growth in your Christian walk see the 22-page Bible study *Basics for Believers* by Jim Berg (BJU Press, 1978).

APPENDIX D

1. This appendix article is copied directly from *Taking Time to Quiet Your Soul*.

INDEX

Adam and Eve 66, 73, 82
ADD. 142
addictions 4
adrenaline. 6, 45–48
anger 3, 35, 48–49
   definition of 48
   rooted in unbelief 37
anorexia nervosa 30, 36, 45, 132
anxiety 3, 35, 43–48
   definition of 43, 48
   disorders . . 45–48, 147–53
   synonyms. 43
authority 106–7

Baker, Henry W. . . . 64–65
belief. 66
   definition of 13
benevolence. 73–75
Bible . . 37, 39, 93, 96, 123–24,
130
   study . 119, 126–28, 155–56
bipolar disorder . 49, 50, 54, 140
bitterness 3
body 6, 23, 46–47, 49
   disciplined 24–25, 28
bulimia nervosa 45, 132
Burroughs, Jeremiah 63

Carson, Alexander 107
Charnock, Stephen . . .102–3
chastening. 116
Christian liberty . . . 66, 119
Christlikeness. 86, 116, 118–20
church. 93, 107, 128–29
Clinton, Bill. 81
conscience. 4
consequences 81–82
contentment 59–67
   definition of 63
   Paul's testimony of . 60–62
covetousness 65–66
creation 104–5, 113–14
cross 77–79, 100, 138–39
cutting. 148

David 64, 81, 84
depression . . . 30, 49, 141–42,
147–48, 152–53
despair. 3, 35, 49–50
   rooted in unbelief 38
diagrams
   bridge. 23, 25, 29
   the way down 35
discipleship 8, 118
discipline 28, 125–29
discontent . .35, 40–42, 65–66
   definition of 40
discouragement 3

disintegration 14, 35, 37
drugs, pychiatric
   See medications, pychiatric
emergency. 46–47
entertainment. 4, 48
Epaphroditus 60–61
evangelism 79, 88
excellence 72–73
exercise 47

failure 97–98
faithfulness 93–101
   stabilizing truths. . .19–20
Fall 85, 100
fantasy. 12–13, 39
fear 43, 79, 86
   rooted in unbelief 37
   See also Anxiety
fellowship 7, 83
forgiveness. . 16, 26, 81–82, 97
frustration. 3

glorification 86
glory of God. 15, 119
godliness. 60, 125
God-ward gaze 6–7
goodness. . 72–75, 86–87, 102
   stabilizing truths. . .16–18
good news 138–39
good Samaritan 82–83
government 106–7
grace. 39, 65, 75
   stabilizing truths. 18
greatness
   stabilizing truths. . .18–20
greed. 4
guilt 4, 26

hatred 3
hell 83–84, 137–38
holiness 77, 97
Holy Spirit . . . 88, 125, 155
hope 66
hopelessness. 49
humility 9, 60, 75

idolatry 69–70, 73
illumination. 124, 156
illustrations
   Aeneid 98
   birthday party . . . 116–17
   bridge. 22–29
   child's artwork 76
   Diamond Head. 105
   directional gyroscope . . .
   91–93
   emergency room 83
   gold rush 120

"good" roommate . .72–73
   jets 6–7
   lost and found 138
   lost contact. 123
   marriage 38
   Old Yeller 84–85
   plastic fruit. 60
   raquetball 125–26
   Santa Claus 12–13
   Tinker Bell the cat. . 71–72
   tombstone 67
   VW bug 118–19
   wallet pictures 69
immutability 93
infallibility 112–13
infiniteness . . 95–96, 111–12
Israel. 100, 129
   captivity of 84, 93
   in the wilderness . 41–42, 66

Job 15, 102, 114, 116
Joseph 109
joy 66

knowledge. 111–17
   of God 11, 15, 67
Kushner, Rabbi Harold . . 102

loneliness 97
love 70–80, 115
   stabilizing truths. . .17–18
   subset of God's goodness. .
   72–75
Lucifer. 66
lust. 4, 27
   for more 41, 66

medications, pychiatric. .30–31,
50, 54, 140–46, 148–50, 152,
154
meditation. 8, 123–25
   MAP method of . . 155–57
   of a worrier. 45–46
meekness 8–9
mercy 81–89
   definition of 82–84
   subset of God's goodness. .
   86–87
mind. 22–23
   disciplined 24–25, 28
   renewed . 15, 22, 28–30, 47
ministry 129
Moses 81–82, 95
   unbelief of 37
motives 27

noise. 1, 11
   cure for 7–9, 22

dangers of 6–7
inventory of 2–5
unbelief the cause of . 15, 20
obsessions 4
obsessive-compulsive disorder 45, 140
omnipotence 103
   stabilizing truths 18
omnipresence
   stabilizing truths . . . 19–20
omniscience 112

panic attacks . 23, 31, 36, 45, 54, 140, 142, 146, 148
Paul 60–62, 84
peace 1, 5, 66
perfection 94
perfectionism 44–45
Philippian jailer 61–62
possessions 4
power 70, 72, 102–9
   definition of 103
praise 127, 157
prayer . . . 99, 127–28, 156–57
preservation 105–6
pressure 22–30
   handling biblically . . 26–29
   its effects on the mind and body 23
pride 8
promises 99, 115
prophecy 100
prosperity 60
providence 105, 116
provision 99
pyschiatric disorders
   anorexia nervosa . 30, 36, 45, 132
   anxiety disorders . . 45–48, 147–53
   bipolar disorder . . 50, 54, 140
   bulimia nervosa . . 45, 132

cutting 148
depression . 30, 49, 141–42, 147–48, 152–53
medications . 30–31, 50, 54, 140–46, 148–50, 152, 154
obsessive-compulsive disorder . . 45, 132, 140
panic attacks . 23, 31, 45, 54, 140, 142, 145, 148
   root cause of 37
self-injury 148, 151

Quieting a Noisy Soul . . . viii, 132–33
   testimonies about . 30–33, 50–54, 140–54

reality 12–14, 39
   definition of 12
recreation 4
relationship with God . 38, 122
repentance 15, 127
responsibility 25
rest 6, 122
Rich, Marc 81
routine 128–29

salvation 97
   plan of 137–39
Satan 73
Savior . . . 6, 87, 100, 122–23
self-existence 95
self-injury 148, 151
sexual abuse 31
shame 4
Simeon 100
sin 26–27, 75, 85, 137
slavery 107
sovereignty 107–9
   stabilizing truths 18
spending a day with God . . . 158–60

Spurgeon, C. H. 116
stability 13, 15, 130
stabilizing truths 15–20
stress 6, 22
submission 107, 130
suffering 83–84, 115
sufficiency 64
suicide 14

temptation 41, 155–56
testimonies . . 30–33, 50–54, 140–54
thoughts 1
   "if only" 40–42
   inventory of 3–5
   ours vs. God's 36
   "what if" 43–44
Tozer, A. W. . 69–70, 104, 120
trials 116
truth 36–37
   nature of 11–13
   stabilizing 15–20

unbelief 20, 34–39, 66
   as cause of noise . . . 15, 20
   as root of all sin . . 36–38
   definition of 14
unchangeableness 93–96
   stabilizing truths 19
Uriah 81

Watson, Thomas 60, 64
wisdom 111, 117–21
   stabilizing truths 20
wonder 113–14
Word of God . . . . See Bible
world 5, 39
worry 43–47
   See also Anxiety
worship 79, 114
wrath of God 75, 85